THE DESIGNS OF
ARNE JACOBSEN

Thomas Dickson
Henrik Lund-Larsen

THE DESIGNS OF
ARNE
JACOBSEN

Interiors, Furniture, Lighting and Textiles
1925 – 1971

PRESTEL
Munich · London · New York

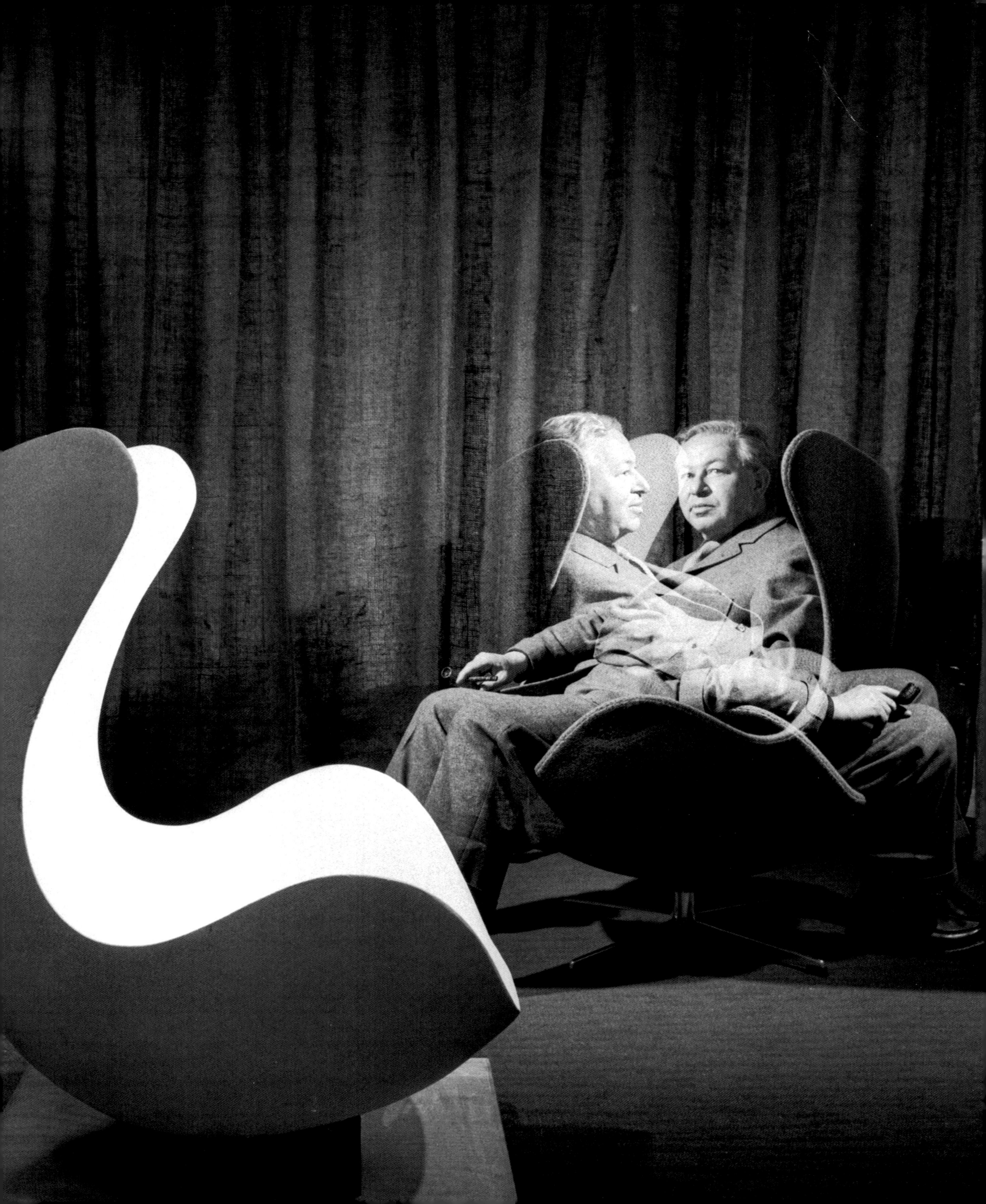

Arne Jacobsen was caught between Apollo and Dionysus – between architecture and design. In professional circles, and especially in Denmark, Jacobsen is known as one of the most successful architects of the 20th century. But on the broader international stage, it is probably his furniture that comes to mind when people hear the name.

The books written about Jacobsen to date tend to describe him as a building architect who also happened to design furniture, lamps, door handles, and the like for his buildings. But the picture is far more nuanced than that. Dig a little deeper, examine the sources, and study his incredibly numerous and versatile works, and you'll see how a picture emerges of a dedicated creator who may well be one of Denmark's first true industrial designers.

This book is the story of an architect who was one of the most far-reaching and productive innovators of his generation. Had he just concentrated on designing buildings, he would still have been awarded a prominent place in the architectural hall of fame. Yet with incredible diligence and ingenuity, he also created a design landscape consisting of hundreds of unique products and designs. That said, he didn't draw everything himself, which we'll touch on later in the book. Indeed, one of his greatest strengths was serving as a leader, motivator, and curator for the many employees and organisations with which he worked. Moreover, he had an almost seismographic ability to sense the spirit of the times. This did not make him a turncoat, however, but rather an artist who intuitively understood what so many needed and craved. Such as when he and his wife Jonna, during their exile in Sweden in the Second World War, began drawing, painting, and producing textiles with nature motifs. It was at that time that such material struck a chord with people, as most longed for a more peaceful and safer world amidst all the horror and misery.

Later, Jacobsen would create some of the distinctive furniture, lamps, and other industrial products that represent the cool Danish-Nordic design of the post-war period.

How he saw himself was that of an architect and not a designer – the latter of which he considered an English buzzword that he loathed. In interviews, Jacobsen often referred to classical Roman architects such as Palladio and Vitruvius, while his modern references were Gunnar Asplund and Mies van der Rohe. He described design, on the other hand, primarily as something functional. "This little chair is good for small apartments," he said of the *Ant*. "This is an ice bucket, but at home we use it as a soup tureen, as we eat more soup than we drink spirits" – he was, of course, talking about the *Cylinda Line* series.

Not least inspired by Nietzsche, the Greek gods Apollo and Dionysus were often referred to at the Royal Danish Academy of Fine Arts and in architectural circles, and so was Jacobsen.

In this context, Apollo represents the god of cool aesthetics, while Dionysus was the god of feasting and wine. Architecture of the 20th century, and art for that matter, was often seen as a battleground between the pure, beautiful, and objective Apollonian form on one side, in accordance with the functionalist mantra "form follows function", and then the unbridled and expressive Dionysian culture on the other. Jacobsen's *architecture* can be seen as Apollonian, cool, and clear, while his design is more playful and atmospheric. In the hierarchy of art history, long-lasting architecture was perceived as being higher than the changeable and innovative design, which was seen as pop.

Jacobsen believed that a better world could be created through architecture and, to this end, agreed with most contemporary architects on this point. His buildings are subdued – they were not yet so innovative or outlandish in their expression, but created for the spirit of the times. When a change occurred in the 50s, Jacobsen followed suit. And while he speaks reverently of Apollo's virtues, it is really Dionysus whom he worships from this point on – full of lust for life and desire. And it was at this moment that Jacobsen, somewhat to his own surprise, "hit the mark". He found himself at the forefront and was anything but low-key during this period.

Throughout his career spanning over four decades, he had an unparalleled ability do this again and again, with buildings, design, and textiles – 400 buildings, 150 textile patterns, 100 furniture designs, and no fewer than ten major product collections that all became his life's work.

Arne Jacobsen in a
sailor's outfit on the
right together with
Mogens and Flemming
Lassen on the far left.

The great train robbery. *The architect Flemming Lassen, his brother Mogens Lassen (also an architect), and Arne Jacobsen knew each other from school. All three had been sent to boarding school in Nærum for having been a touch too restless at home. So restless that they stole a train for fun and made off with it. They must have had fun.*

They were three teenagers with a passion for technology who had read stories about how to drive a steam train, build an iron bridge, dig a canal, and make loop-the-loops with an aeroplane. So it was their shared boyhood dream to take a train for a spin. And it was just a matter of putting the theory to the test. They had poured over the American magazine Popular Mechanics. *Like them, it came into being at the beginning of the 20th century.*

So when they found water and coal on board the engine parked up at Lyngby Station late one evening, and the two little carriages coupled to it put up no fight, all that was left to do was to turn the regulator and various other valves. But hey, when you release the brake, the train moves – that much they definitely knew. It's one thing to start a train, and quite another to bring it to a stop. Several kilometres further along the small side track, they finally managed to turn the right handles in the right order and bring the engine to a stop. However, they couldn't resist a single, small farewell whistle from the steam locomotive when they arrived at the final station in Nærum. The following day, the morning train that was supposed to leave Lyngby was missing. Passengers for the large industrial buildings along the line couldn't get to work and the police were called – a train robbery had taken place.

It was the little whistle that gave the three lads away. And they went to school in Nærum, did they not? Thankfully, they were let off with a stern talking-to thanks to the intervention of the school and parents – they were just boys being boys. A little burdened by guilt, but probably also quite uplifted, the whole train-driving experience ignited something in them that night. It was the feeling of mastering the technology that was necessary to tackle the modern world. They weren't fully aware of this at the time though, of course. But, following their share of mediocre high school exam results, it was this "wow" experience that steered them towards technical school and then onto architecture school. The three simply weren't content with burying their heads in books.

In the early 1920s, while the world was still reeling from the aftermath of the First World War, the three friends learnt about old-world aesthetics and architectural art atthe Royal Danish Academy of Fine Arts' School of Architecture. They measured column chapiters in temple class with their teacher Kaj Gottlob, studied residential construction with Ivar Bentsen, and designed storage furniture under Kaare Klint. In these years, modern architecture and design were primarily seen as a refinement of earlier decorative developments in the historicist style. The ornaments and decorations were removed, but the basic models, buildings, and furniture had the same shapes and proportions as always.

So even though modernism slowly found its way into new designs, perhaps a little fumbling and hesitant at first, it nonetheless rested on a solid classical foundation. In particular, this involved mastering the fundamental elements of all good architecture and design – the carefully balanced proportions, the expert use of colours and materials, and the almost musical mastery of the structure, and the rhythmic flow of the objects.

Arne Jacobsen was born on 11 February 1902, the only child of Johan and Pouline Jacobsen. His father was a wholesaler of buttons, snap-fasteners, and safety pins. His mother was one of the first women in Denmark to be educated in banking. In her spare time, she had a passion for flower painting. Jacobsen's childhood home was located on Classensgade in Østerbro, Copenhagen. It was old-fashioned and bourgeois in the historicist style of the time. As a child, he was very lively, one could even say restless, which resulted in him being sent to boarding school in Nærum from the fifth grade onwards. He was no star pupil, but one of his teachers discovered his talent for drawing and painting, and she encouraged him to continue by giving him a box of painting supplies.

At boarding school, Jacobsen met the Lassen brothers, Mogens and Flemming, with whom he remained good friends and colleagues for many years. They encouraged him to pursue an architectural profession early on, as Arne's father opposed his son going down the artistic route that he otherwise wanted to. Johan Jacobsen believed it to be an uncertain and unfulfilling profession. However, Jacobsen's talent for painting, especially watercolours, benefited him throughout his career. His refined and seductive technique was able to produce the illustrations that later became so famous and iconic. These were often instrumental in his ability to win architectural competitions and convince a client of the excellence of a construction project.

Longing to expand his horizons, and perhaps also as a reflection of the restlessness of his childhood, Jacobsen went to sea at the age of 19, where he sailed for a short period as a mess boy on an ocean liner serving the route between Copenhagen and New York. Once back home, Jacobsen began preparing to enter the Royal Danish Academy of Fine Arts. Lacking the right diplomas, his path to admission to the School of Architecture took Arne to courses at a technical school on Ahlefeldtsgade in the Nansensgade district of Copenhagen. The courses included practical training which, in Jacobsen's case, meant spending some time over those years as an apprentice bricklayer during the summer periods. In connection with his studies at technical school, he also worked as a bricklayer in Germany for a summer. In so doing, he learnt so much German that it became his preferred foreign language from then on, even when negotiating with clients in the UK.

While Jacobsen studied at technical school, he also worked at the Hjejle and Rosenkjær design studio before graduating in 1924 and being admitted to the Royal Danish Academy of Fine Arts' School of Architecture that same year. At that time, it was still significantly characterised as being a classically-oriented faculty, with the modernism of the new era only slowly making its way through. Like all other students at the time, he was introduced to the various branches of the architectural profession, in addition to the obligatory classic school of thinking. During his time studying here, Jacobsen came into contact with the architect Kay Fisker, nine years his elder, and who was then a teaching assistant and docent at the Royal Danish Academy of Fine Arts. In 1925, Fisker hired Jacobsen as an assistant to work on the Danish pavilion for the World Exhibition in Paris which, as far as is known, showcased the first example of independent work from Jacobsen's own hand – a chair – which even won a medal on the same occasion.

At technical school, Arne met Marie Jelstrup, whom he married in 1927 – the same year he graduated from the academy. Their engagement and subsequent marriage brought Jacobsen closer to artistic circles and the culturally radical elite of the time. Marie Jelstrup and her sister Estrid, inseparable friends, were women of the world. They had had an eventful childhood, seeing large parts of the world aboard their father's steamship. He was a captain, and at that time it was not unusual for captains' families to accompany them on long-distance voyages. The family was from the Faroe Islands and the sisters' cousins were the authors William Heinesen and Jørgen-Frantz Jacobsen.

Jacobsen became part of this culturally radical environment, which he happily participated in, at least initially. Here he met several other cultural figures of the time. Estrid, Marie Jacobsen's sister, had been briefly married to a Brit, taking the surname Bannister. She is the seductive woman portrayed as Barbara in Jørgen-Frantz Jacobsen's 1938 novel of the same name. Curiously, the book features a rotund, money-loving, ladies' man, Gabriel, who is based on the persona of Jacobsen.

Jacobsen naturally also knew Poul Henningen – both for his lamps and the magazine *Kritisk Revy*, which Henningen headed for the few years it was in circulation from 1926 to 1928. Henningen wrote lots of articles for all sorts of newspapers and specialist magazines, not least the debate and criticism columns; indeed, he once gave Jacobsen's *Forest Snail* wicker chair from 1929 a rather lukewarm review. Later, in the autumn of 1943, the two men crossed paths once again when, fleeing Nazi occupation, they rowed themselves and their girlfriends to Sweden.

The architect, professor, and writer Steen Eiler Rasmussen got to know Jacobsen even before his time at the Royal Danish Academy of Fine Arts. Their families lived in the same building on Classensgade, and while Jacobsen was attending technical school, it was arranged that Rasmussen would give him some extra tuition in mathematics. Rasmussen was good in maths, whereas Jacobsen struggled. However, the arrangement never really worked out, either because Jacobsen was completely hopeless or Rasmussen was a bad tutor. Later, a more serious matter would arise in their relationship.

In 1940, Rasmussen wrote a book about modern Danish architecture for a German publisher, and strangely enough, Jacobsen wasn't mentioned in it. There has since been speculation as to whether this was due to Jacobsen's Jewish background, and that Rasmussen gave in to editorial pressure to exclude him. This, together with the failed maths lessons, led to great reserve between the two gentlemen, which Rasmussen tried to smooth over a number of years later with a highly adulating letter that he sent to Jacobsen.

After a few years, Arne's marriage to Marie went downhill. He worked hard to make his design studio a success rather than just allowing it to tick over. Many hours were spent drawing proposals for architectural competitions and cultivating the important connections that could lead to new commissions. He neglected Marie, and especially their two sons. However, there had been bright times in their marriage, including during several extended trips abroad and not least the classic educational trips to France and Italy. The journey to France in the late 1930s saw the family's car transported by steamer to Antwerp, then driving on to Paris and back through Nazi Germany. Before that, they had also been on an extended trip to the Soviet Union, which, oddly enough, took place in the middle of winter, and which apparently did not have a specific professional purpose for Jacobsen. He shot a lot of films in black and white on this trip, none of which focused on architecture. In fact, it was ordinary life that he depicted in an almost ethnographic manner, including some excellent portraits of the furrowed and weather-beaten faces of older Russians. Before he left, Jacobsen held meetings with the Soviet ambassador to Denmark – perhaps hoping for construction projects in the country?

By the early 1940s, Arne and Marie's marriage was coming to an end. The villa on Gotfred Rodes Vej was remodelled slightly so that the couple each had their own bedroom, which ultimately led to separation and divorce. It seems that Jacobsen never really felt at home in his wife's culturally radical circles. He was raised more traditionally, and although he could have a laugh and join in the festivities, his goal in life was to succeed professionally – not to change the world.

When looking at an artist's work over a long life, we usually do so from a distance or start at a particularly fruitful period of that person's creative life. In this way, their previously created works can be understood and recognized as part of a process on the path towards the later highlights of their career. Likewise, one can see the later unfinished and unrealised projects as falling within the realm of possibilities, as something that could have become even more fantastic and made their life's work even greater had they seen it through.

In Jacobsen's case, it's important to bear in mind the difference between the slowness of architecture and the speed of product design. A large building complex can take more than 10 years from when the pen first hits the paper to completion. Or, it may even come to an untimely halt in the project phase due to lack of finances or waning support. After all, a design rarely takes more than a couple of years and usually results in production.

To understand Jacobsen, we have to look at how he worked and how he acquired his commissions. His working life fell into three phases, through which he evolved from local architect to global master. He fostered different fields of activity throughout these phases of his career, but we can also see how his interests all centre around three main topics – design, architecture, and textiles.

Flemming Lassen and Arne Jacobsen were childhood friends from their time at Nærum boarding school. Both graduated as architects from the Royal Danish Academy of Fine Arts, along with Flemming's brother, Mogens. Especially in their younger years, Flemming and Arne often worked together, usually on competition projects. Here they are relaxing in front of their first joint success *The House of the Future*, which was built as a mock-up for the Forum 1929 exhibition. Flemming Lassen on the left in a Mies van der Rohe tubular steel chair, and Jacobsen in his own chair, nicknamed *Forest Snail*.

Here are Jacobsen's complete construction drawings for his own villa on Gotfred Rodes Vej. Many of his early works were drawn on a single sheet of paper. At that time, houses were built based on technical drawings like these, along with numerous visits to the construction site and the carpentry workshop. Details were discussed and decided throughout the development process.

In the early 1930s, Jacobsen was firmly rooted in Gentofte, which at that time was being developed from a field into a residential area. Here he cultivated a good and rich network of master craftspeople and was active in Rotary Club circles. These networks gave rise to commissions, and even bigger construction projects such as Bellevue and thus other residential developments fell onto Arne's desk in this way. He worked on all his commissions in the design studio that he had designed as part of his home. He could draw anything and took on any commission, from the window decoration of a florists to a development plan in Jægersborg. Such were the working conditions of all architects back then. They were, in essence, small grocery stores with their own home upstairs and the business in the basement, and of course, where the wife helped out.

Jacobsen was talented, enterprising, and intuitively understood where things were headed and where he could get commissions for his design studio. He was a man who saw and seized the opportunities that presented themselves, and he pursued any avenue that yielded profit. In the early 1940s, the in-demand architect was busy with large projects in Aarhus and Søllerød, but was also grappling with some major personal challenges. As mentioned, he divorced from his wife Marie and was forced underground as an alleged communist, especially following his trip to the Soviet Union, and at one point had to flee his homeland as a Jew.

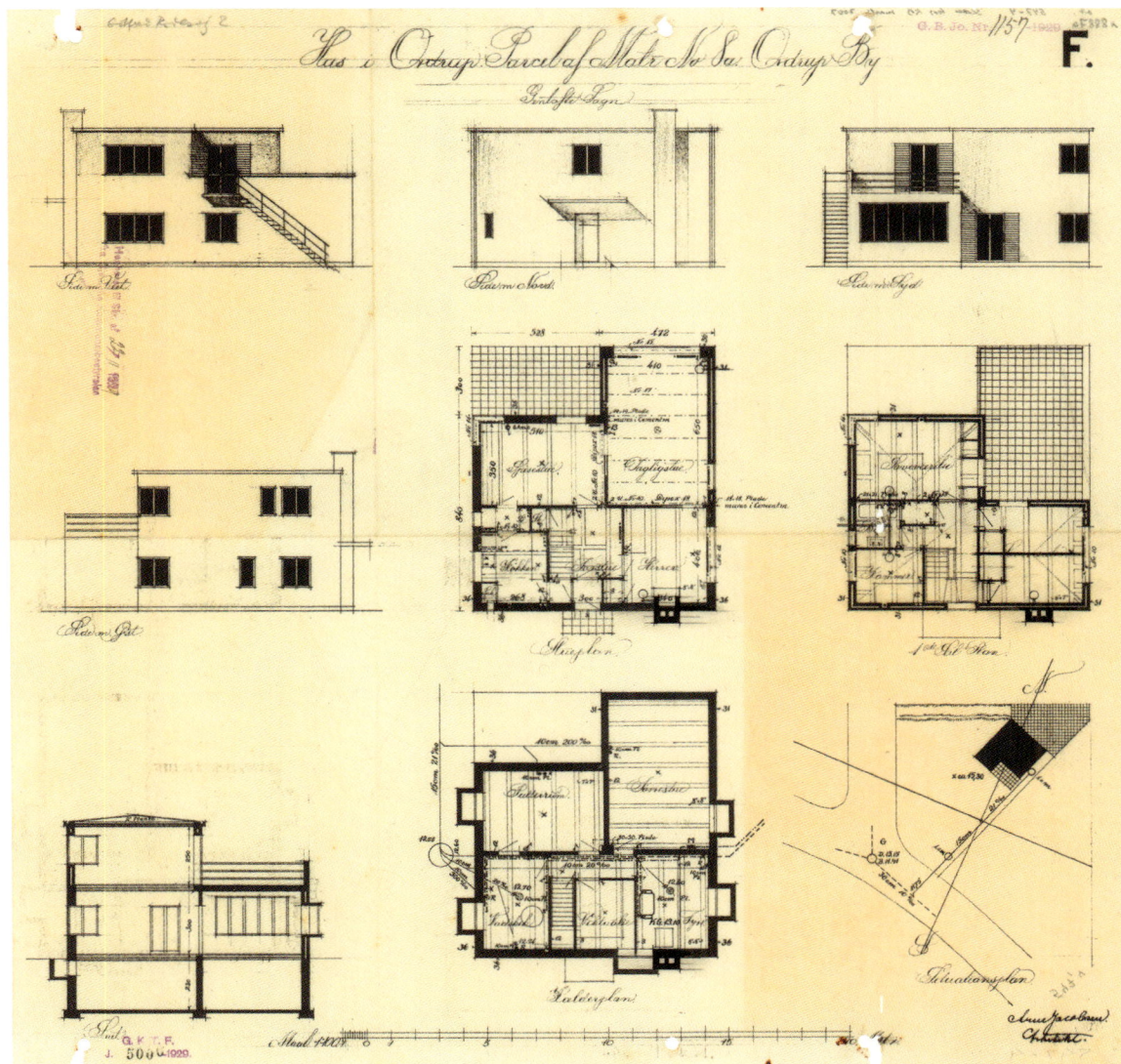

In the shadow of war, Arne took a break for reflection. It could be that he was experiencing depression. In any case, he took things down a notch or two with work. But unlike so many other architects who faced involuntary idleness, Jacobsen truly blossomed in exile. His focus became his large textile collection, which helped him survive financially. It was created through close collaboration with his second wife Jonna, who was a trained cotton printer and textile designer. They lived in Stockholm for a good 18 months and eventually got married there.

Returning from Sweden, he was on top form and ready to get back in the saddle. His initial houses and sketches following the end of Nazi occupation arguably show a return to the modern Nordic-Romantic style from before the war, but with the building of his own new house just after 1950 and with the next decade spent working across Denmark, it is in this period that the architect and designer we now know so well developed. He had become aware of his style through the application of a convincing design language – he had entered into character. However, the shortages and restrictions that persisted in the wake of the war meant that it was chairs and textiles that kept him afloat through to the mid-50s. Things finally started to take off in Denmark and West Germany, and in 1960 he was able to inaugurate his famous masterpiece, Copenhagen's Royal Hotel. It had been 17 years since he had designed the equally magnificent town halls of Aarhus and Søllerød.

In the 1960s, in collaboration with Otto Weitling and Hans Dissing, he developed his design studio. It was now more international in nature with large building projects in countries including India, Pakistan, Germany, Sweden, and the UK. Jacobsen's design studio had become one of Denmark's largest and expanded out of the basement of a townhouse on Strandvejen in Klampenborg into a huge villa on Svanemøllevej in Hellerup, and with smaller temporary branches in other places where it seemed worthwhile.

It is during this period that Jacobsen's major product collections have their roots: *Vola*, *Cylinda Line*, the tabletop series, the lamps for Louis Poulsen, and new furniture series for Fritz Hansen. It is also here that his architectural design language develops in leaps and bounds. The 1950s saw two trends – the yellow-faceted bricks and the curtain wall boxes. Examples of the brick buildings are Munkegård school from 1956 and his own townhouse from 1951. Similarly, the Royal Hotel from 1960 and Rødovre town hall from 1956 were buildings with curtain wall facades. These were structures with non-load-bearing glass-clad facades that were clearly inspired by similar American buildings – almost carbon copies, in fact.

In the 1960s, Jacobsen's buildings took several stylistic turns. These turns were of course based on experience and a well-proven design language, and the curtain wall look was further refined. However, the redeeming feature was that this type of building could take on a raft of different looks. The first project to break the mould was St Catherine's College in Oxford from 1964, which brought with it a new brutalist style, where emphasis is placed on the structure's supporting and supported elements. The final projects of the decade evidence how he moved with the times and built in more of a space-age style – this can be seen in the Danish embassy in London and the unrealised proposal for the Roskilde University Center. Some of his furniture designs also became much more loose and fashionable.

Now in more of an industrial context, he revisited the qualities that brought his earlier works together into a gesamtkunstwerk in the 1930s, where everything was created for the specific building and based on craftsmanship. However, he only just achieved this before his death in 1971.

The professor's table in the large dining room at St Catherine's College.

Alvar Aalto receives an invite to dinner

There's a fire in the fireplace in the master bedroom. You can hear rustling from the kitchen. Marie Jacobsen is putting the rabbits in the oven – they shouldn't be in for too long. The guests have all arrived now. Kay Fisker and the slightly younger couple Eva and Nils Koppel have settled into the living room. It's a collegial dinner; the network needs to be nurtured. Nils and Eva are invited as they have connections to the company's main prospect, who should actually have arrived by now: Alvar Aalto. The master architect is probably just a little late making his way out from the city.

In the ultra-modern, functional house that radiates modernity from the outside, they sit in front of the fireplace in furniture that was probably designed by the master of the house, but in a classic style that exudes bourgeois and solidity. Fine woodwork, French wicker, and soft cushions. Designed a few years earlier, but with references to the English furniture tradition a century beforehand. It's cosy, with lots of plants and the large grand piano as the centrepiece, which Marie is playing. The boys are put to bed.

Meanwhile, the conversation turns to architectural fees with Kay Fisker and Jacobsen accusing each other of undercutting. They're both involved in large, prestigious projects in Aarhus – the university and the city hall. The public spotlight is firmly on the two gentlemen, both of whom have gone below the tariff to secure these attractive assignments. By the time construction is complete in a few years, they will have both taken a substantial step up into the super league of architecture. It is therefore also annoying that their god, their role model, and their standard-bearer cannot keep to an agreement. Nils Koppel calls the hotel. Alvar Aalto is sitting at the bar, he is told.

His ears are glowing as red as the embers in the fireplace. "Well, I did go slightly under the fee," says Arne. "Fortunately Erik and I got a little extra for designing the tower." Kay Fisker admits: "Yes, if the brickworks hadn't donated all the bricks, we wouldn't have been able to build the university." Where Kay Fisker and CF Møller's university is intended to express Danish values, with yellow bricks and distinctive tiled roofs set in an open landscape, Jacobsen has taken a different route. The town hall, now with a tower, is intended to express a modern administration building in an opulent material – marble. Unfortunately, the cargo ship carrying the marble sinks, and new Norwegian marble has to be obtained – this was just before the brick building was plastered white.

The rabbits are now overcooked, and Marie is angry. She thinks this is a silly men's dinner. Where has he got to? Nils Koppel calls the hotel again – Alvar Aalto is still holding court at the bar. Koppel persuades a waiter to coax Aalto into a taxi.

Finally, after several hours, the hero arrives. He's a tall, handsome man who speaks charming Scandinavian – when he's sober. Which he isn't. The dinner's a mess, but Aalto's charm soon brings Marie around. They gather around the table, and Aalto tells of his achievements and praises the gentlemen who are on their best behaviour in the company of their esteemed guest. The happy scene is short-lived, however when, after an hour, Aalto collapses on the sofa and starts snoring. Nils Koppel orders another taxi. Goodnight, dear Alvar Aalto. See you again soon.

A friendship had nevertheless been established, and Eva and Nils Koppel then travelled to Helsinki from time to time to visit Alvar Aalto, work in his studio, and get inspiration. Moreover, Jacobsen received a good deal of help from Aalto when he was in exile in Sweden, and Kay Fisker and Alvar Aalto relied on each other in organisational contexts in the international architectural community.

After a few years employed by the city architect in Copenhagen, and before that as an assistant at the World Exhibition in Paris in 1925 with the slightly older Kay Fisker, Jacobsen established himself as an independent architect. Even before his 30th birthday, he had five villas built before designing and building his own on Gotfred Rodes Vej in Ordrup in 1929. He in fact 'built' two versions of his house: a realistic square one that looked like white concrete but was actually plastered brickwork, and a fantasy futuristic round house that also looked like white concrete, but was made of cardboard.

The square one was his own, equipped with a porthole in the entrance door and an external steel ladder, just like on a ship. His wife Marie must have felt at home here: A reminder of the voyages on the seven seas by steamship that she made with her family as a child. The house had all the modern amenities with a toilet and shower. It boasted a flat roof and steel windows, which all functionalist houses had to have back then. In addition, there was a garage and conservatory, and not least the large modern roof terrace above the living room:

All elements that indicate the dawn of a new era. People of yesteryear would consider it a waste of time to spend time on a terrace with the aim of getting a tan – and not just on the face, but on the whole body. Where once the desired skin colour of the bourgeoisie had been pale to distinguish themselves from the tanned working class, the ideal now became a brown complexion. Sunburn and exercise were healthy, and this could be seen in the new houses with their emphasis on light and air. The houses had to look as healthy as their casually dressed residents.

1929 was the breakthrough year for functionalism. The Bauhaus school had become the darling of the media. French architect Le Corbusier's predictions that the home was a machine to live in had become a reality. Although Jacobsen's modern house was plastered and painted white to look like concrete, his interior didn't follow the fashion. The interior of the house was cosy, consisting of heirlooms and the architect's own designs – the first touches of furniture in an English colonial style. The chandelier in the dining room and pleated curtains expressed a certain traditional style with roots in the tassel-rich Klunke era of the late 19th century. As he said himself: "I find that old furniture looks great, even in new living rooms, but of course there will be some homes where you have to shave off the worst of the clutter."

Arne and Marie Jacobsen's house on Gotfred Rodes Vej in Ordrup. The house was built in 1929, and the photo was taken before the garden had time to mature and the house still stood in a neighbourhood that was yet to be fully developed.

Drawing of Arne Jacobsen's and Flemming Lassen's *House of the Future* from 1929, which was built as a 1:1 mock-up for a large construction exhibition in Forum the same year. The house was in the new functionalist style, which was promoted by the Bauhaus school in Germany, among others, but it was also a fantasy design, boasting the latest technical achievements of the time, such as the large antenna designed to be able to receive electricity wirelessly.

However, these typical curtain tiebacks and tassels of the Klunke era certainly didn't make the cut in the round *House of the Future* which Jacobsen designed together with his childhood friend and fellow student Flemming Lassen for the great building exhibition in Forum in 1929. It showcased all the instruments that the future would soon bring. Both the architectural breakthroughs and the technological innovations. The teenage fascination with technology, fostered by the American magazine *Popular Mechanics*, had a long-lasting impact on the two young men. Their winning entry in the *House of the Future* competition was a truly functionalist house, complete with plenty of gadgets and features that, in many cases, had barely made it off the drawing board.

The design did well at the exhibition: A round house that tracked the sun's path across the sky, and a doormat that was replaced by a grate fitted with a vacuum cleaner that sucked visitors' dirt away from the soles of their shoes with a loud whirring sound. However, their proposal for inflatable furniture was rejected. Steel pipe furniture sent a clearer signal about the direction in which this era was headed, and when you couldn't get hold of originals from Germany, you could build them from water pipes. An antenna on the roof that could receive power wirelessly was also created, as well as a gyrocopter. Being able to land on a small cross on a flat roof was a fascinating idea, and the roof could also be used for sun worship and sports, among other things.

The construction exhibition, which only lasted a week, catapulted the careers of these two young architects, who sat and drew in the master bedroom of Jacobsen's new functionalist house in Ordrup.

At sea, on water, and in the air seems to be the motto for *The House of the Future*. After all, there was a garage for a car and a boat, along with a landing pad for some kind of helicopter. It was a technology that was yet to be developed, and that's probably a good thing considering the whirlwind it would create when it landed among the sunbathers on the terrace. However, the romantics Lassen and Jacobsen couldn't help themselves. As in a classic country house, ivy crept its way up the facade and fine flowerbeds and clipped hedges were planted in the garden. The cool Bauhaus style is not really implemented to its fullest.

A sketch and working drawings for the hearse that Arne Jacobsen and Flemming Lassen drew won the competition in 1930. The two also designed a coffin blanket, for which they received third prize in the same competition, which was held by the Danish Cremation Association. The vehicle was criticised for looking like a race car. However, it did result in Jacobsen being contacted a few years later by Ford's factory in Sydhavnen and asked to come up with suggestions for vans.

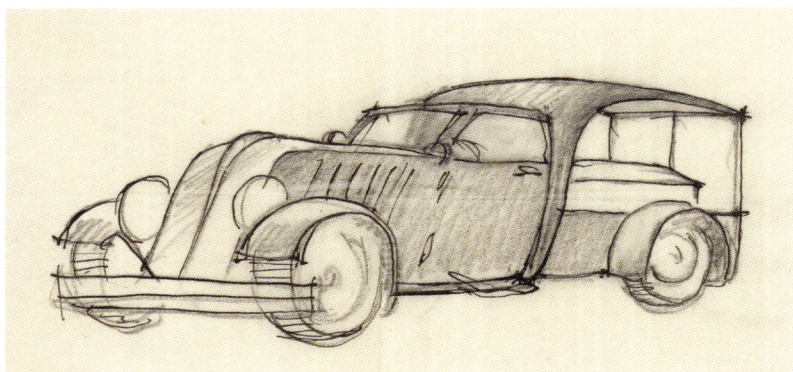

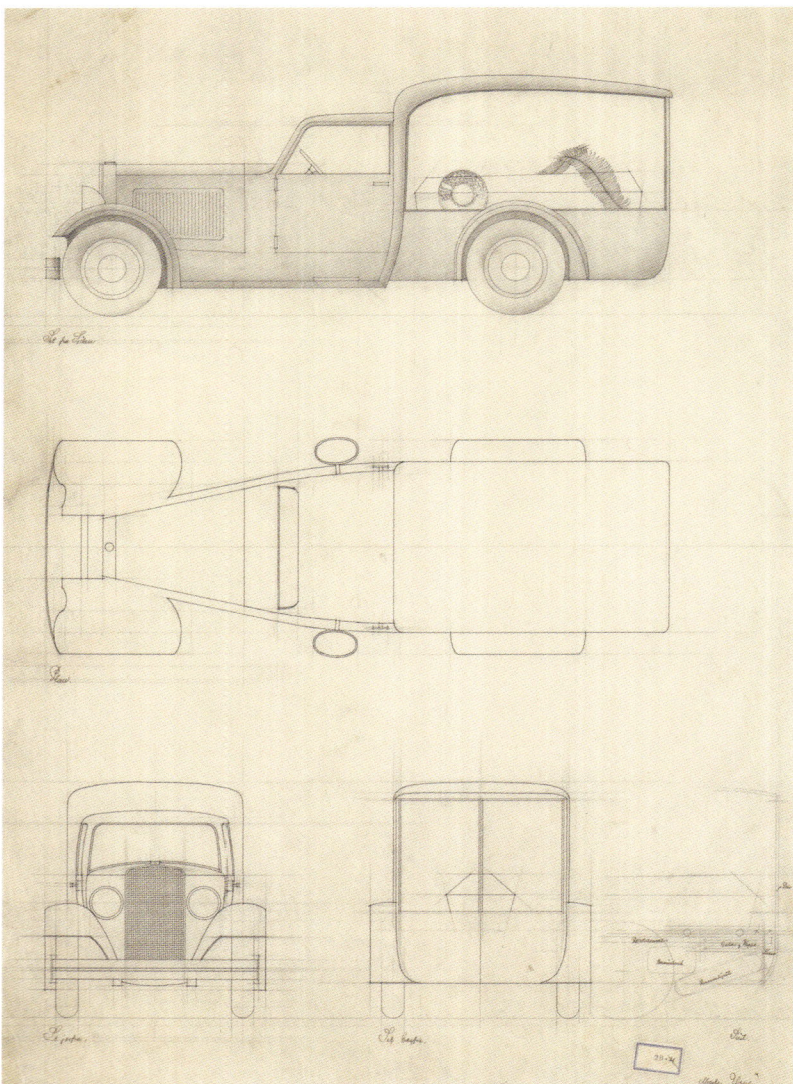

What is a modern and radical architect to do if they want to make a living from their newly opened practice? First of all, they must find somewhere strategic to settle down, in an open plot surrounded by plenty of building space. Of course, this should be north of Copenhagen, where the wealthy wanted villas – right here, right now. Then you join the Rotary Club to create a network of master craftspeople, lawyers, wholesalers, and preferably a mayor.

Within a few years, Jacobsen became Gentofte's favourite local architect. It may well be that he had radical ideas and yearned for the functionalism that he'd seen at Bauhaus in Dessau and at the Stockholm Exhibition in the summer of 1930. But he had to make a living, so villas in yellow and red stone with gable roofs became his most used style in the local area. He came to count several such villas as neighbours to his own white one. And if the lady of the house really wanted a half-timbered house, Jacobsen skilfully drew slender birch trees in the foreground on the drawing for the sales prospectus to give a sense of a post-and-beam look, and the architect could then go back to his colleagues knowing he hadn't compromised.

Jacobsen's network was beneficial. His own white villa soon had a design studio wing added. A partition wall was erected across a window to split the children's room in two. He soon landed commissions with consortia for the construction of multi-storey buildings throughout the municipality. The most famous is Bellavista, and then there's the top of Jægersborg Allé where it joins Lyngbyvejen, where almost an entire town was created, designed by Jacobsen. Vangede and Skovshoved also had proposals drafted, although neither were implemented. Instead, bathing facilities were built in Charlottenlund, Klampenborg, and Dragør. Using a construction system from Junckers aircraft factories, he built a badminton hall and concrete riding and tennis halls. In an attempt to boost his career, he tried to get an observation tower built in Klampenborg or Charlottenlund, but without success.

However, none of this was enough for the enterprising architect for whom nothing was too small and nothing was too big. He entered competitions for everything from cigar equipment to airports and city halls. In the mid-1930s, the all-in-one architect was born. An architect who took care of everything, from buildings to design, which would later come to provide a healthy income from royalties. Perhaps this was something he was already aware of in 1929, when the small amounts dropped into his account for his first mass-produced products, the *Forest Snail* garden chair from the company Wengler and the *Codan* lamp from Louis Poulsen (now known as the *Bellevue* lamp).

Arne Jacobsen's and Flemming Lassen's next joint project was a competition for something unusual … a hearse. Granted, it was fashionable for cars to feature a design. Walter Gropius and Le Corbusier did the same, and Danish Kaare Klint designed cars for his brother Tage, who was director of Denmark's largest car factory at the time, Triangel, located in Odense. The car was no longer an up-and-coming product and had matured into a mass-produced consumer good, albeit still only for the wealthy and still mostly built by hand. With elegant, streamlined shapes, they designed their hearse so that the funeral could take place in style and at unprecedented speed. Jacobsen then received an offer from Ford Denmark to design vans, although it is not known whether anything came of that request.

Jacobsen was busy with his many villas. Flemming Lassen helped out – sometimes as a partner, other times as an employee at the design studio. In 1932, they participated for the first and only time at the Carpenters' Autumn Exhibition. Once again, they took a punt with something new: The modern American film and interior design dream, as seen in Hollywood movies. The box-shaped furniture with white faux leather – which could easily be confused for Le Corbusier's famous designs – were more suited to exhibition use than as actual home furnishings, and therefore the stylistic expression of these pieces of furniture was quickly abandoned by the architects in their subsequent works. The bamboo furniture was more of a success. Individually, they had begun designing furniture in woven bamboo for Copenhagen basket makers, including Wengler. This beautifully curved and lightly crafted furniture had a clearly modernist style. They were joined by a third architect, Viggo Boesen, who added another string to their bow with his *Fox* chair.

An architectural collaboration could now begin, starting with Jacobsen's design studio. Arne Jacobsen, Flemming Lassen, Erik Møller, and Viggo Boesen entered competitions together, often in pairs. They worked with the same furniture manufacturers – bamboo furniture maker Wengler, and upholstered chairs by cabinetmaker A.J. Iversen. Flemming Lassen designed his armchair *The Tired Man*, and Viggo Boesen supplemented it with his *Little Petra*. Jacobsen's many examples of upholstered furniture of that time were produced by Littmann and Rud. Rasmussens Snedkerier, which was also his usual supplier of interior details and furniture for the buildings.

Flemming Lassen and Arne Jacobsen entered competitions for several town halls, as well as for Copenhagen Airport. They secured the commission for Søllerød Town Hall, which was eventually built. Furthermore, Erik Møller single-handedly initiated the competition for Aarhus City Hall. Jacobsen asked if he could join, and together they won. Both Aarhus City Hall and Søllerød Town Hall were built simultaneously. Flemming Lassen and Erik Møller won the competition for Nyborg Library, which was built at the same time as the town and city halls. Flemming Lassen, Erik Møller, and Viggo Boesen finally entered a number of competitions together. Although they were awarded prizes, none of the entries came to fruition.

Arne Jacobsen and Flemming Lassen continued to collaborate on competitions throughout the 1950s. Alongside his own design studio, Flemming Lassen worked on a competition for a school in Vangede together with Arne Jacobsen, and he was an employee of Jacobsen on the Rødovre Town Hall project and the later extension of Søllerød Town Hall, which was mainly Flemming Lassen's work. The individual architects' studios were quite small at this time, despite winning large commissions. Accordingly, the approach was to enter into partnerships. Later, after the war, when Jacobsen had matured as an architect, it appears that his design studio became a slightly more permanent organisation with him as sole helmsman. At least that's how it worked in the 1950s. In the 1960s, Otto Weitling, the associate partner, largely took care of the German projects.

A town hall and a city hall

By the end of the 1930s, Jacobsen, along with the majority of Danish architects, had abandoned early modernism, at least its smooth white concrete aesthetic. This was certainly a feature of Jacobsen's own house on Gotfred Rodes Vej from 1929, of the Bellevue buildings built between 1931 and 1937, and of the gas station on Strandvejen in Skovshoved from 1937, which he designed for Texaco. Although the 1937 Stelling House on Nytorv in Copenhagen had hints of the same rounded and clean expression, its colour and large square tiles covering the facade made it slightly different. These buildings, along with the factory buildings for Novo Industries, drew heavily on inspiration from the German art and design school Bauhaus and the Swiss-French architect Le Corbusier.

From 1937, a new chapter began in Jacobsen's approach to architectural expression. A more independent Nordic architectural style took shape, which could be seen not only in the choice of materials, but also in the abandonment of the building's rounded styles in favour of sharper shapes. Aarhus City Hall and Søllerød Town Hall, both designed in the late 1930s, are the best examples of this. They are similar in many ways – not least their cladding made of Norwegian marble slabs and characteristic low sloping roofs.

↓ Søllerød Town Hall, completed in 1942, which Arne Jacobsen and Flemming Lassen won the competition for in 1939. Like the city hall in Aarhus, the crystalline box features windows that sit shadowless on the very edge of the marble facade. The roof edge is a chamfer of the facade and was originally made of marble. It was replaced with copper for better durability after a few years.

→ Aarhus City Hall. This time Arne Jacobsen worked on the project with Erik Møller. They won the competition in 1937, and the building was inaugurated in 1941. It is more classical in its design than Søllerød with large halls and long corridors ending in beautifully curved staircases. In this watercolour, we can see the entrance foyer with the council chamber jutting out on top and a tower in the background adorned with the city hall clock. Later in the construction phase, the clock was moved down to the middle of the tower to give everyone a better chance of reading the time.

The long office wing at Aarhus City Hall. The equidistant repetition of the wall lamps is a principle that Jacobsen would come to use many times in his career. Here they also mark the office door locations.

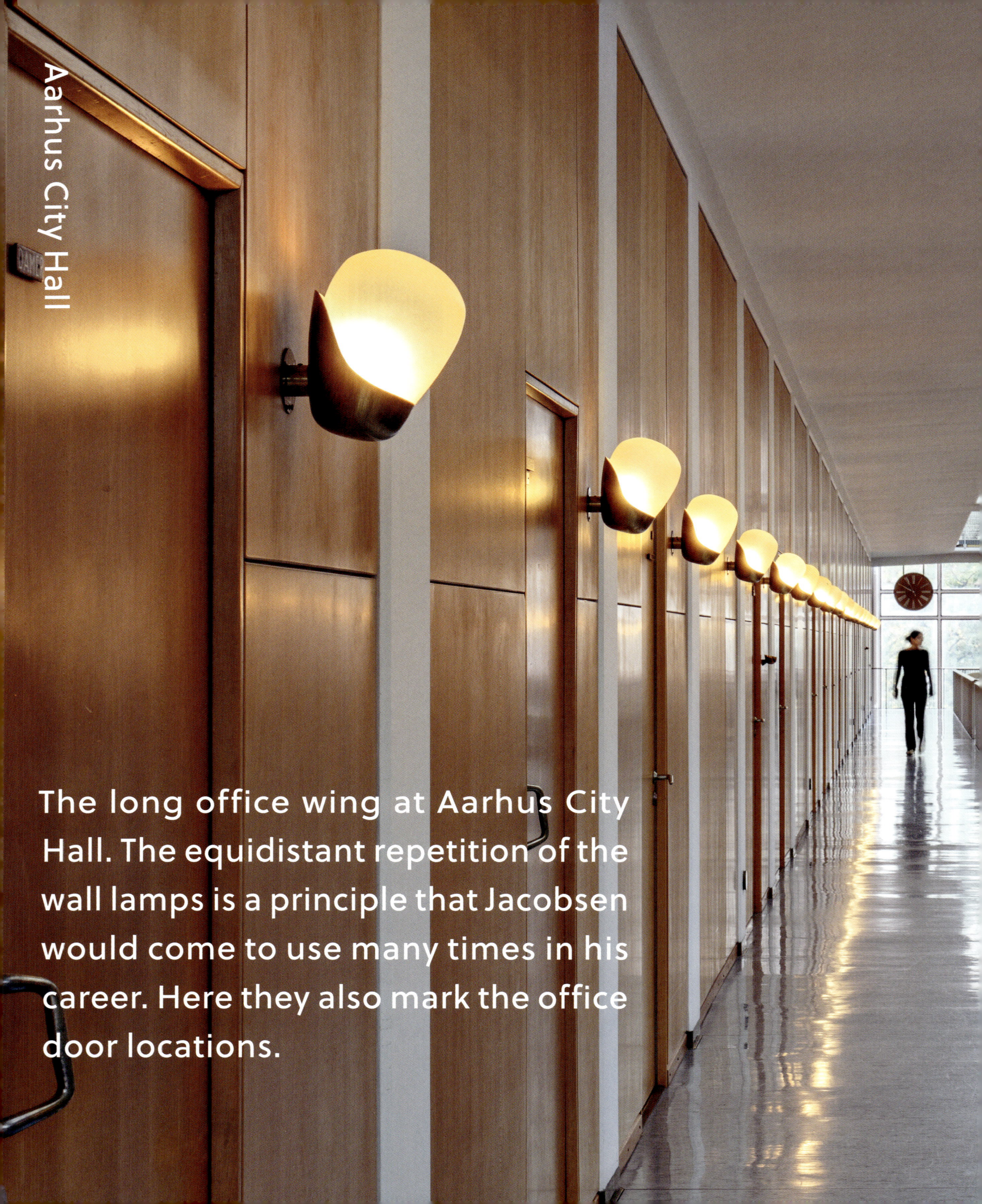

One of the many clocks designed especially for Aarhus City Hall, which can be found in several locations around the building. In the background is the giant, movable carpet that can be used as a partition between the entrance foyer and the lobby. Below you can see the pattern of the carpet when extended.

The interior of Aarhus City Hall hints at the involvement of furniture designer Hans J. Wegner in the project. On the recommendation of Orla Mølgaard-Nielsen, his teacher at the Danish School of Arts and Crafts, Wegner was hired by Jacobsen and Møller to assist with the interiors. Wegner moved to Aarhus with his wife Inga to work in the small, makeshift design studio housed in a separate building next to the construction site. In addition to Erik Møller and Wegner, there were a couple of young architects. Inga was hired as a secretary at the project office, while Jacobsen remained in Copenhagen.

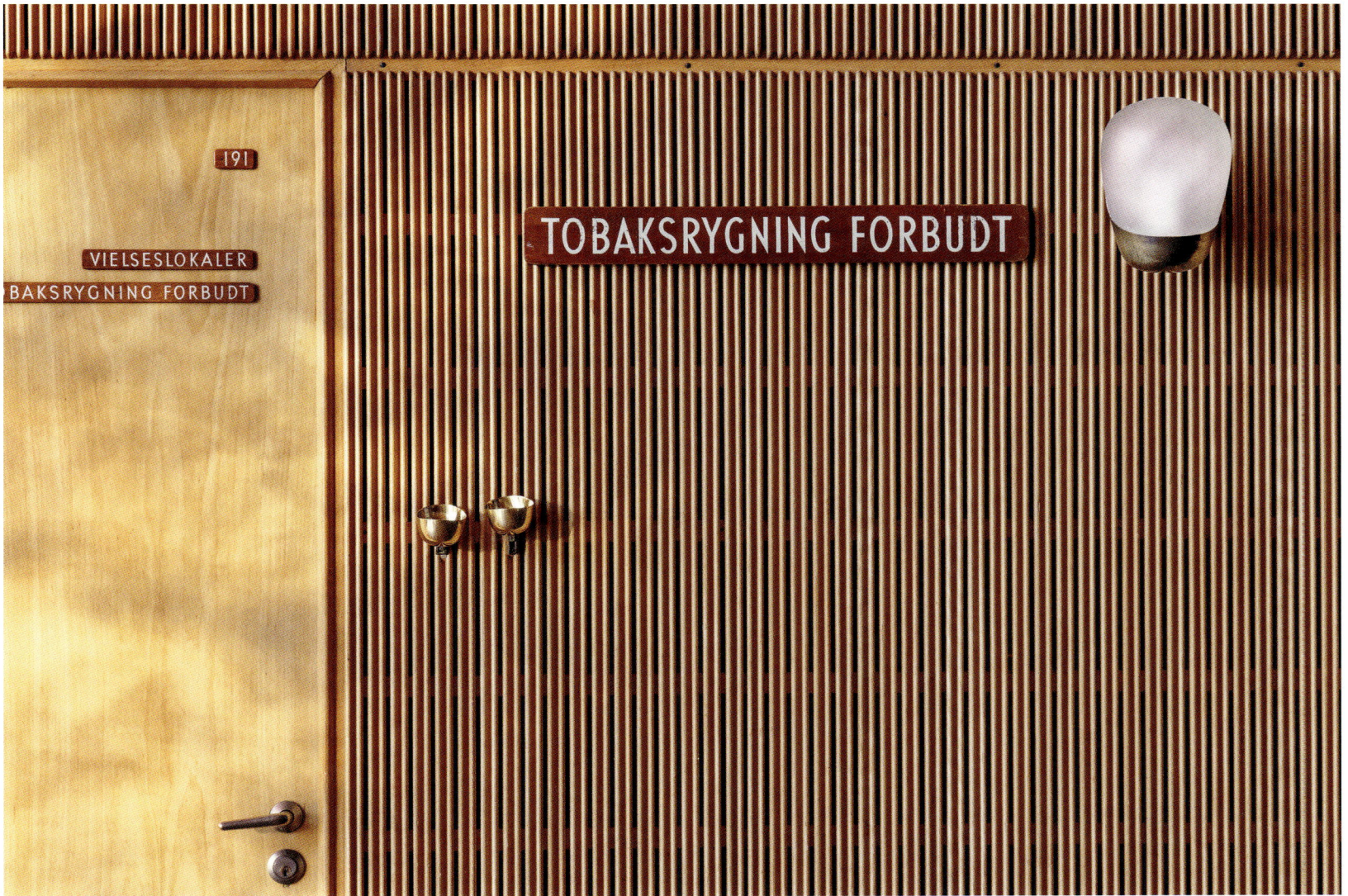

Above is a section of one of the corridor walls facing the lobby. It features a characteristic wall covering and typical wall lamp used throughout the building. The signage has remained in its original design and, despite the more recently added "No smoking" sign, the original ashtrays still exist throughout the building. At the bottom is the special control panel for the elevators, which was also designed especially for the building.

→ → Facing the high-ceilinged lobby are corridors that provide access to meeting rooms and the council chamber. Here, in addition to the doors, wall lamps, and consistent use of wooden slat wall coverings, we can also see the special hexagonal pendant lights that are unique to the building.

The interior design of the city hall was a complete package, where virtually every detail was the subject of a unique architectural process. There was a tradition that larger, prestigious buildings were taken care of by the architect from start to finish, with specially designed furniture and other furnishings. Aarhus City Hall boasts a whole range of tables and chairs, fixed counters, wooden panel wall coverings, signs, clocks, lighting, and more, all designed as a collaboration between Jacobsen, Møller, and Wegner. This practice culminated in Jacobsen's design of the SAS Royal Hotel (now Radisson Collection Royal Hotel) in the late 1950s, St Catherine's College in Oxford in the early 1960s, and the National Bank in Copenhagen a few years later.

The exquisite craftsmanship of the furnishings at Aarhus City Hall is thanks to local carpentry company Plan Møbler under Wegner's supervision, although the design style does not seem quite as modern as the building's architectural expression. It is as if the modern influence from the south has affected the architecture more than the furniture and other design elements. This may be because the method of production reflects the artisanal traditions as were frequently exhibited at the Cabinetmakers' Guild in Copenhagen at that time. While new technologies were creeping into the external appearance of buildings, especially given the development of concrete, interior design elements and in particular furniture, lagged behind somewhat. There was still something classic about the interior design.

Wastepaper basket, which, like almost all of the furniture and furnishings in Aarhus City Hall, was designed specifically for this building. The profiling of the walls is repeated as a motif in the wastepaper basket, this time in rosewood.

One of the comfortable armchairs. The comfort level varies from chair to chair. From the simple and relatively uncomplicated waiting chair for the public that can be seen on the opposite page, to the armchair, where one sits in comfort to listen to the exchange of political views.

Part of one of the
corridors, which also
shows one of the chairs
designed for the many
offices and meeting
rooms in the city hall.

← From the anteroom
to the council chamber,
showing the delicate
treatment of the interior.

→ → The wedding chamber
with the grey-painted
chair-and-sofa series.
The influence of Hans
Wegner is clear, such as in
the motif with the wicker
back that is so uniquely
Wegnerian, just like his
rocking chair for FDB
Møbler from the same
period. In the background
is the original wall
decoration by Albert Naur
of wild flowers painted
directly on the wall, which
also inspired Jacobsen's
textiles with bouquet
motifs such as *Autumn
Flowers* and *Vines*.

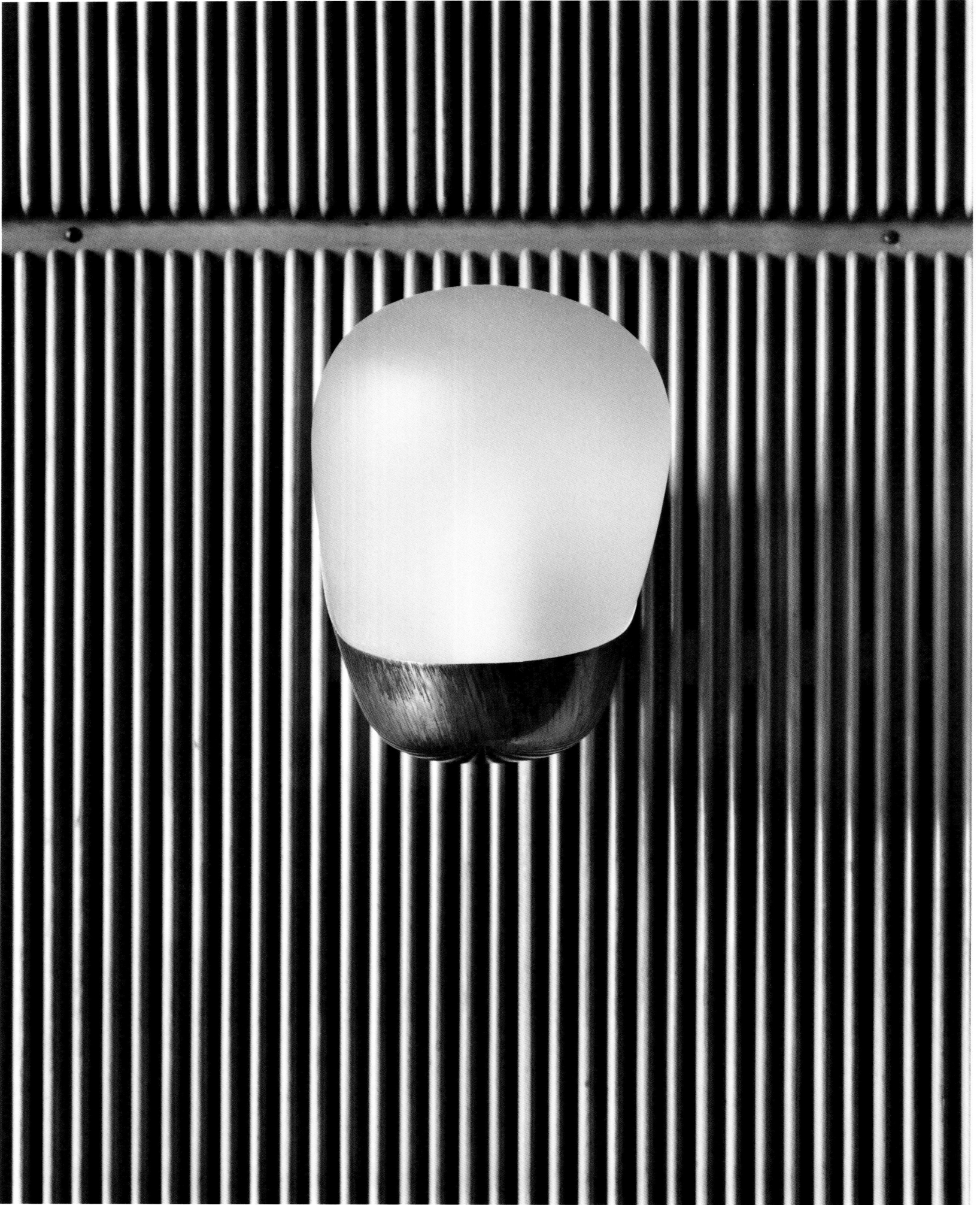

← Wall lamp used in the building's semi-public areas, hallways, and corridors. It is typical of the period and is somewhat reminiscent of lamps that other architects of this period designed for their building projects, including Vilhelm Lauritzen's Radiohuset in Frederiksberg in Copenhagen.

The long welcome bench in the foyer. It serves as a discreet barrier to the city hall's many rooms and also as a welcoming gesture. If you needed to wet your whistle before pleading your case to an official, you could take a sip from the tap in the copper basin in the middle of the picture.

↑ Detail of door with fine joinery and the door handle that was designed specifically for the city hall.

↓ One of the larger meeting rooms, located on the ground floor next to the lobby. The room can be divided into several smaller rooms using a bi-folding wall. Once again, an unmistakable Wegner imprint has crept in with the rustic spindle-back chairs.

↑ The council chamber's pendant light with 'floating' reflector shade. In the background are the audience seats on the balcony.

Wood became the dominant element inside Aarhus City Hall. The panels on most walls are made of veneered boards or as mouldings. Herringbone parquet was laid on much of the floors, while all movable chairs, fixed counters, and other furniture are all examples of fine joinery. For example, the fixed benches in the open areas, which in this context seem to be some of the most modern, were delicately made of shaped wooden slats. Even the clock faces that formed the background for the numbers and hands were made of veneer. All very nice, but quite detached from the ultra-modern design that Jacobsen came to represent in the post-war period.

↓ One of the many meeting rooms at the city hall, equipped with comfortable upholstered chairs – certainly for longer meetings. The lamps are fairly simple glass pendants that are mostly designed to light up the entire room.

↑ A small waiting area in the foyer, just inside the main entrance.

→ → The council chamber with its unique floating lighting, soundproofing veneer on the walls, and a huge carpet on the floor, showing a stylised map of Aarhus Municipality. The chamber's chairs are upholstered in quilted leather.

← One of the original wall-mounted ashtrays found in large numbers at the city hall. The acorn shape is found again in the lamps.

→ The audience seats on the balcony above the council chamber are evocative of a cinema.

A small selection of the many pieces of furniture that were designed in connection with the fitting out of Aarhus City Hall and produced by local carpentry company Planmøbler. Several pieces continued in production after the war with a few changes, but now with Hans Wegner as the designer.

There are several versions of armchairs that were designed for the city hall. This one was used in the canteen, among other things.

Armchair used in the council chamber. The seat and back are in leather, with the city's coat of arms embossed into the back.

A standard chair that was, and still is, used in many places in the building's offices and meeting rooms. Braided leather seat with a wooden back.

A standard chair, but in a slightly wider version and with armrests.

A desk chair with swivel base, braided leather seat and back.

Stacking chair for placing in rows at events in the foyer, for example. Note the coupling brackets mounted on the underside of the seat. This chair is inspired by Sven

Markelius's *Orchestra Chair* for Helsingborg Concert Hall, which was completed in 1932. Arne Jacobsen and Sven Markelius were good friends.

As mentioned, several different chairs were designed for the city hall and its offices, meeting rooms, and council chamber. Nowadays they seem quite ordinary and rather traditional – made of solid wood, with or without armrests, upholstered in full grain leather or textile, sometimes braided with webbing. Desks, conference tables, sofas, and cabinets, etc. were also of good quality, but not overly modern. Signs, clocks, doorknobs, and similar small items were solid in design, but not avant-garde. The wall lamps, placed in abundance in corridors and common areas, were akin to those from Vilhelm Lauritzen's large buildings, Radiohuset and Kastrup Airport, both designed in the second half of the 1930s, than to Poul Henningsen's lamps, for example. The same applies to the suspended hexagonal glass lamps in the lobby, which in retrospect appear almost old-fashioned.

↑ The typography, like other furnishings, was designed specifically for Aarhus City Hall and has since been preserved and is used in the production of new signage for the building.

↓ The large curved spiral staircase that runs from the ground floor to the basement level.

All in all, it seems as if the consortium, consisting of Jacobsen and the other architects wanted to create a relatively subdued version of modernism – a new kind of Nordic functionalism – rather than continuing in a radical functionalist style like the one that had prevailed in the interwar period. However, they also followed a certain international trend that was characterised by a more monumental style, which could be seen most clearly at the World Exhibition in Paris in 1937, where several countries, especially Germany and the Soviet Union, built pavilions in a much more formal and classical style than had been seen for many years. Aarhus City Hall and Søllerød Town Hall were a bit of a transitional phenomenon with their marble facades and copper roofs. The period that followed became more regional with a greater focus on the use of brick, which can be seen quite shortly after in Kay Fisker and C.F. Møller's Aarhus University and later in Jacobsen's new townhouse development on Strandvejen in Klampenborg from 1947 to 1951, which he himself moved into.

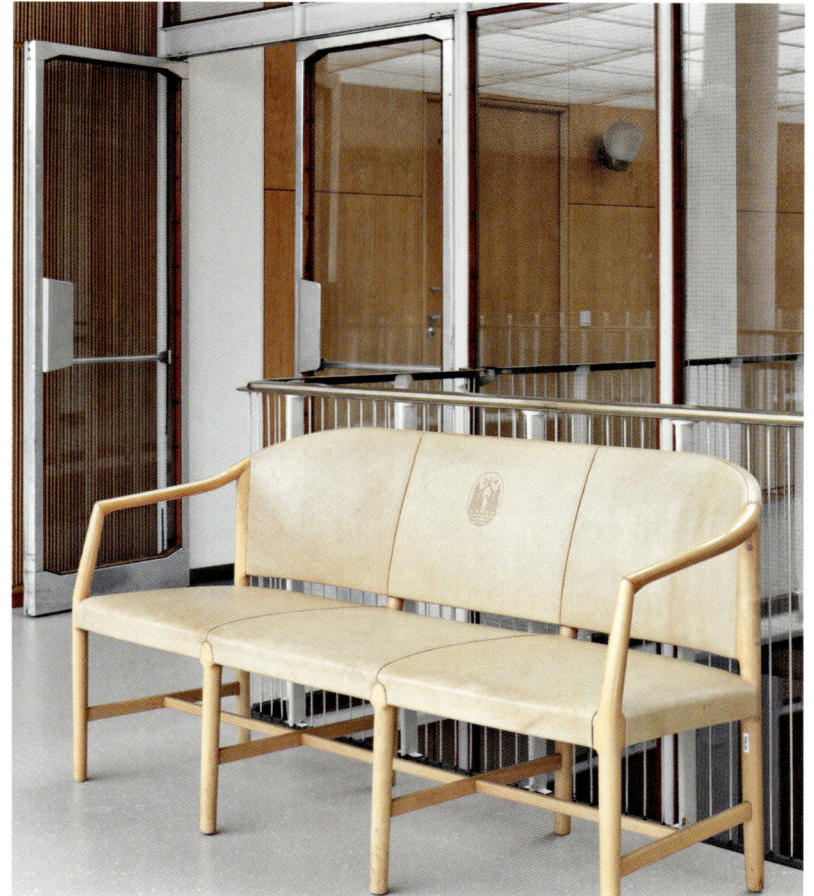

↗ A three-seater sofa on one of the upper floors on a landing facing the entrance foyer.

↓ Congregation area at the city hall. The string of offices runs along the foyer's corridors, and this is also where you will find the elevators.

The council chamber in Søllerød Town Hall seen from the audience balcony. Its interior has changed substantially. The large oval shade in the ceiling is both a sound reflector and hides the lights that provide indirect ceiling lighting. The original interior is now packed away and stored.

← Older photo from Søllerød Town Hall, giving a glimpse through the swing doors to the original canteen.

The construction of the town hall in Søllerød started in 1939, two years after Aarhus city hall. Although similar in many ways in terms of materials, shape, roof construction etc., Søllerød Town Hall was designed by a different team of architects and designers. This time, Arne Jacobsen teamed up with Flemming Lassen, while the furniture, lighting, and other accessories were designed with assistance from furniture architect Aksel Bender Madsen. The furnishings here were mainly manufactured by Rud. Rasmussens Snedkerier in Nørrebro in Copenhagen, and is very similar to what was designed for the Aarhus project, only perhaps not as liberated and independent due to the influence of Wegner.

← Door handle at the main entrance of the town hall.

↓ An older picture from the council chamber with the original furnishings, which were less pompous than at Aarhus City Hall.

→→ Seating set in undyed leather featuring a sofa, table, and armchair in the municipal director's office. The sofa is one of two original examples that were designed for the now-removed wedding hall. At the time, no one thought about producing more, but 80 years later it is in series production by the Danish company &Tradition. The seats are upright with minimal padding, perfect for the bride and groom as they wait nervously for the mayor.

Since the design of the furnishings formed part of the overall construction contract, the furniture differed from site to site, and was manufactured only in the desired quantities by local carpenters. They started from scratch every time, and the architects designed new furnishings for each building, because it was part of the total architectural fee. In order for the interior design and furnishings to be of a quality and aesthetic equal to the effort put into the building itself, a furniture architect was often associated with the project, making Hans Wegner much sought-after during these years. He produced countless examples of furniture, lamps, and other furnishings in just a few years, all original and of extremely high quality. It is clear how this work left a mark on his subsequent production.

← Looking out onto the landing through the double doors that lead to the council chamber's audience balcony. Note the small, fixed leather sofa found on each floor for impatient citizens as they wait.

↗ Meeting table furniture set in an office equipped with a hand-blown glass pendant light. The pendant was produced by Louis Poulsen for a number of years. The chairs are similar to those from Aarhus. It is a standard chair from Fritz Hansen.

→ Wall lamp designed especially for Søllerød Town Hall, which was primarily located in hallways and stairwells.

→→ The council chamber's audience seats with a sound-dampening back wall. In the foreground is the long table with accompanying chairs, which was once designed for the now-defunct wedding room.

Four chairs that were designed for the town hall in Søllerød Municipality in the early 1940s. Arne Jacobsen and Flemming Lassen partnered on the project with furniture architect Aksel Bender Madsen as an employee.

The chair is made of rosewood and comes from the original wedding room.

Armchair with leather
upholstery and part-
upholstered armrests.
Used as an office chair
and at the meeting
tables in the executive
offices. We get a sense
of a completely different
design language here
compared to the furniture
in Aarhus – it is more
mobile and not quite
as rigid.

→→ From the audience
seats on the balcony in
the council chamber. The
writing indicating the
press locations is original
and has been retained in
many places throughout
the building.

The original armchair
from the council chamber,
fully upholstered, but in
the same style as the
chair above.

Reserveret

← Doors leading out from the balcony of the council chamber. Elegantly veneered with signage in italic script and a wall clock that resembles the one designed for the city hall in Aarhus a few years earlier. Through the door you can see a rather special wall uplighter.

↓ Meeting room on the ground floor with the classic armchairs, glass pendant lights, and original colour scheme.

→→ Staircase landing with the glass-encased elevator. In Søllerød, the pervasive metal – aluminium – gives a clear modernist and industrial expression.

← Swing doors leading from the landing into the meeting room hallway and audience area of the council chamber.

↓ Wall clock, designed for the town hall with a veneered face and Roman numerals. Especially refined is the centre of the clock face that arches outwards, raising the hands.

↓ Aluminium wall lamp that illuminates the hallway via a reflective oval glass plate. It was also used as a work lamp by turning the lamp housing over and mounting it on a pole. A similar approach was used at Stellings Farvehandel, as can be seen on the next spread.

The decorating store Stellings Farvehandel was completed in 1937. It was solely Jacobsen's work and so he reused earlier designs. The chairs at the counter have a Bauhaus-like look, perhaps with a bit of American influence. They have a chrome-plated steel frame, and a similar design was used for the bar stools in the restaurant at Bellevue, albeit with a more ornate backrest. Meanwhile, the opal glass pendant light in Stellings borrows its expression in part from the large pendant light in Aarhus City Hall, albeit on a simpler scale. See page 52.

Where did you go in the 1930s to buy a table and four chairs for the dining room? To the carpenter, of course. Just like if you wanted a suit, you went to the tailor who made it according to your measurements. Most consumer goods were made to order according to the customer's wishes and measurements. Factory production of these product groups was still in its infancy, almost non-existent. All furnishings for the home were handmade by a carpenter on a bench using hand tools.

When Jacobsen and his partners made canteen chairs for Aarhus City Hall and Søllerød Town Hall, and when he also needed chairs for his sports buildings in Gentofte and Emdrup, they were all independently designed and made to order. Apart from Hans Wegner and Plan Møbler subsequently selling variants of the Aarhus furniture under their own names, none of the chairs from these three projects would go into series production. On the other hand, Jacobsen did not use his machine-produced Novo furniture from Fritz Hansen, which he could easily have placed in the buildings. The reason must have been that there was greater profit in designing furniture and having it executed as part of the building contract than in receiving royalties from a chair that had already been designed.

Essentially, Jacobsen's art of seduction culminated in the sales room, where the final agreement between the customer and salesperson would take place. Here, the customer was met by a counter with service professionals standing behind it. Around this counter, Jacobsen created elegant break-out spaces for customers, who could wait their turn in built-in or freestanding armchairs while perusing the store's offerings until the salespeople on the other side of the counter were ready.

Sales rooms were a fleeting phenomenon, and sadly none still exist and so cannot testify to how great a master of interior design Jacobsen was. Although gifted architects and designers have designed prestigious business premises for famous brands on a grand scale over the years, in some cases resulting in unforgettable interiors, most have unfortunately been forgotten and lost to posterity.

Jacobsen didn't design many such interiors, and one might even say that the industries for which he designed them were not the most exciting – bank premises and Stelling's shop for drawing supplies. That said, they were a change from the municipal offices, which he also furnished with as much finesse as possible, and so commercial premises received his special attention to transform them into welcoming and well-designed environments. For these premises, Jacobsen drew some of his best pre-war designs.

It was likely Rud. Rasmussens Snedkerier, which was responsible for the furniture and furnishings contract for these commissions. Rud. Rasmussen was certainly Jacobsen's preferred collaborator on such projects. They also fitted the kitchen and built-in cupboards at Jacobsen's home on Strandvejen after the war.

Stelling's drawing supplies shop – located at street level in the modern Stellings Hus, which Jacobsen completed in 1938 – and the few branches of Landmandsbanken designed at the same time, offered a degree of elegance rarely experienced. From the beautifully patterned floors to the curved lines of counters, not to mention the upholstered furniture that provided islands of tranquillity in the centre of the rooms. Exquisite woodwork, finely polished and varnished. And then we have the metal worker's finely crafted brass piano lamps to illuminate the workplaces. Finally, the curved lines of the inviting upholstered furniture testify to a design language that would be repeated in the *Swan* and the *Egg* 20 years later. It is easy to see that this motif was the beginning of what Jacobsen would later come to create on a large scale and with unrestricted international elegance with his Royal Hotel. The future of his design language was already taking shape.

← The Klampenborg chair. A solid chair with a hint of Chinese design, and a stretched leather seat attached under the side struts. A chair with quite a character, which remained in production at Fritz Hansen for a number of years.

↙ The large restaurant, adjacent to the Bellevue Theatre, was a bright room with clear references to the popular restaurants that were shown at the Stockholm Exhibition in 1930.

Conversely, the accompanying bar and lounge were more intimate. The restaurant only lasted a few years before being converted into exclusive housing.

The lounge remains preserved in a small restaurant.

Fritz Hansen was one of the only furniture manufacturers to have sensed that the market would move towards cheaper prices through mass production. Accordingly, the firm acquired the general agency in Scandinavia for Gebrüder Thonet's famous caféfurniture, which had just started being mass-produced. They therefore sold both the 100-year-old classic Viennese chairs and the brand new Mart Stam cantilever chair in steel, wood, and wicker. The furniture was manufactured under license at Fritz Hansen's factory in Allerød. Here, they built up expertise in working with moulded plywood and steam-bent solid beech. It was the older Fritz Hansen who had the vision and ingenuity to find several new patents and methods in a desire to produce new and inexpensive types of furniture.

In 1933, his sons Søren and Poul Hansen became part owners and members of the management team. Søren Hansen was the extrovert who negotiated with architects about possible collaborations, and a competent designer in his own right. Poul Hansen, on the other hand, was the insightful production man at the factory. They were a perfect match for the development that the factory was about to embark on, namely the mass production of its own furniture. Jacobsen worked closely with the factory in connection with the large Bellevue project in Klampenborg. This included the production of the theatre's rows of seats, which were made with Fritz Hansen's new technological breakthrough – moulded plywood. There was also a large restaurant and a bar that needed to be furnished. The most extravagant furniture, typical of the period, was placed in the bar to encourage dancing and flirting with their jazzy frames and backrests. The chairs for the restaurant were different, subdued, but quite characterful with their stretched leather seats and high backs that drew inspiration from Chinese furniture.

↓ In front of the Bellevue complex, Jacobsen designed a beach park with everything it could possibly need, including changing rooms, retail outlets, and a pier for steamers from Copenhagen. The graphics, tickets, and even a special clothes hanger were all included in the overall design package. Out on the beach itself, he set up pop-up stalls with colourful signs. His proposal for a tall observation tower with a rotating restaurant was left on the drawing board, however.

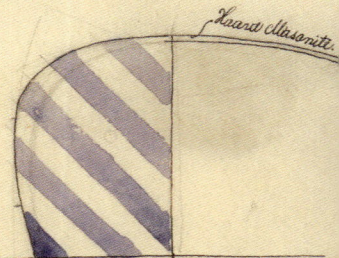

Sidevm Vest.

Set pa Siden.

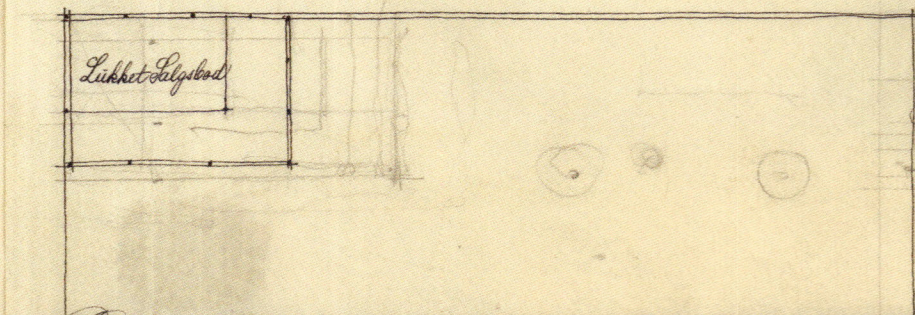

Lukket Salgsbod

Bod til Is og Drikkeva

MAAL 1:50

← Watercolour illustration of the ice cream stand that was built at Bellevue. A quick, simple, and clear drawing. Blue and white stripes and "IS" (Ice Cream) in big red letters – it is summer, after all.

↙ In a sales brochure for Fritz Hansen, Jacobsen presents a sketch proposal for hotel furnishings. It contains beds, cabinets,

and tables, as well as the chair for Novo, which is the only design that ends up being produced.

↑ Elegant curved connecting hallway at Novo with wall-mounted sconces, Italian-inspired chairs, and the special

Jacobsen finesse – the endless planter, filled with plants.

Jacobsen drew inspiration for his chairs from all over the world during these years. At first, he was drawn to British-inspired chairs for his own home and the interiors of his clients' private villas. This was followed by more of a Chinese style for his Bellevue chair before he finished with influences from Italy with the chair for Novo, which was a truly no-frills chair with a wicker seat.

There is an A4 folder in Jacobsen's archive that contains sketches for the furnishings for a hotel. Among the tables, beds, and storage furniture, you'll find the chair which was put into production as the Novo chair. This occurred at same time that his teacher in furniture design at the academy, Kaare Klint, had his Italian-inspired *Church Chair* (later *Klint Chair*) put into production at Fritz Hansen. It far outsold Jacobsen's early chairs and has remained in production ever since. Jacobsen was, it seems, not so concerned with creating chairs for the mass market for Fritz Hansen at this time. For some time, he continued to develop furniture specifically for each individual construction project.

A lamp factory that works with cast metal and Bakelite items and with shades made of extruded metal and pressed glass is, by definition, an industrial company. The items cannot be sanded and individually adjusted like wood. They must fit into the thread when they come out of the automatic lathe. That is the prerequisite for a lamp, of which Louis Poulsen made many. It began in the mid-1920s with the legendary three-shade lamps designed by Poul Henningsen. Subsequently, PH and Louis Poulsen developed this lamp series together and pursued it in many directions, ranging from industrial lamps, sports lighting and the many needs of the home to large chandeliers for public buildings. It was a well-developed modular system that could be varied infinitely. In fact, the lamp went on to evolve into a dental lamp and a greenhouse lamp due to its glare-free qualities.

However, other architects also wanted a slice of the Louis Poulsen pie, and from his early years as an architect, Jacobsen had a lamp in production at the company, or rather a lampshade. It was only the conical lampshade made of pressed sheet metal with a slanted cut that he received royalties from. From the light fitting at the top all the way down to the base, everything else was from Louis Poulsen's stock of standard components. The *Codan* floor lamp (now known as the *Bellevue* lamp) was actually just a generic shade that Jacobsen used, in varying sizes, in several places in his buildings, indoors and out. Such as an up-light at the gas station, or at Stelling and at the Bellevue Theatre, where it was a downlight. Moreover, other architects

such as Finn Juhl and Vilhelm Lauritzen, had designed the same type of lamp, just for other manufacturers, so it was certainly a shape in the style of the time.

Another type of lamp that Jacobsen developed in the 1930s was the elegant wallwasher – a lamp that shines onto the wall. It was quite an expressive lamp, where a circular lamp rod connects the round mounting plate and the domed shade, which was made of either opal glass or metal. This was the lamp that Jacobsen used as hallway lighting if the ceiling wasn't high enough for a suspended pendant. This can be seen in all its elegance at Novo's building in Nørrebro.

The market in the late 1930s was dominated by the opal glass pendant. Every architect had fallen in love with the acorn-shaped lamp in white opalised glass. It was a very useful lamp, gave good light, and was easy to clean. The Jacobsen lamp was created for the offices of Søllerød Town Hall. When he came to furnish Novo's canteen with his Myre chairs in the early 1950s, it was also the lamp he used here, suspended in clusters. It wasn't a lamp that stood out and was actually quite anonymous in its shape.

He developed a more characteristic lamp for the retail premises of Stelling and Privatbanken. A simple and easy-to-read shape – a kind of truncated cone in opal glass, which meant that the lamp could be viewed from the side and thus hang low over a table. It had an elegant appearance and a shape that Jacobsen had taken from the metal pendant lights that were created for Aarhus City Hall.

Jacobsen's first lamp from 1929. In fact, he only designed the shade and received royalties for it. The rest of the lamp is made up of Louis Poulsen's standard components.

At first it only had a model number, before the shade gained some perforations and it was given the name *Codan*.

It remained in production at Louis Poulsen until the end of the 1960s and has since been resumed by &Tradition, now under the name *Bellevue*.

The Charlottenborg chair was probably the chair most clearly designed by Jacobsen in the 1930s. It was inspired by the so-called bucket seats found in the small English sports cars that appeared in the interwar years.

A rearward circular fold with ribs that hold the back cushion in place. This is in turn held together by the armrests, with a bold angle on the front struts to suggest speed. Exhibited at The Royal Academy's annual art fair in 1936.

The furniture from wicker-worker E.V.A. Nissen's workshop were the first designed by Jacobsen to reach a wider audience. The rattan garden chair was, in a way, a breakthrough. In the past, garden furniture was simply a table with heavy benches and chairs around it, where you ate your summer meals. Danes know them as the white furniture depicted on P.S. Krøyer's picture from Skagen with the title "Hip, hip, hurra". Rattan furniture, on the other hand, was different – it was low, less upright, and had a modern look inspired by the Bauhaus design style. Perfect for relaxation, which was the mantra of the new age, helped along by sanatorium pools, seaside hotels, and sport. It was a theme that Jacobsen fostered as an architect throughout the 1930s with bathing facilities at Bellevue, Charlottenlund, Amager Strand, and Dragør. It was a fully developed concept at Bellevue, with riding stables, a restaurant, a summer theatre on the beach, and proposals for an observation tower. Oddly enough, these lightweight chairs were not used here. Nor in Charlottenlund where he built the Hellerup sports club's tennis facility, which was fitted out with heavy upholstered chairs. Yet they could be found in gardens, including his own. There was the snappy Charlottenborg chair, as it was called, which is somewhat reminiscent of a sports car seat, as well as the slightly more geometrically chunky chair, which was given the 'slower' name, the *Forest Snail*. The back angle could be adjusted on the latter, which is made clear by the circular shape on the sides of the chair.

Jacobsen explains to
Sweden's Crown Prince,
later King Gustav VI Adolf,
how a block print works at
the opening of Arne and
Jonna Jacobsen's textile
exhibition at Nordiska
Kompaniet in Stockholm
in the autumn of 1944.

Sweden and textiles

Jacobsen was a non-practising Jew who was aware of his ancestry and in contact with the Jewish organisations in Denmark which had asked him for help for the German Jews after the Kristallnacht of 1938. The Jews had had a tolerable life in Denmark until September 1943. Unlike in other countries occupied by the Germans, they did not have to wear Jewish stars and could move freely – or as freely as was now possible in an occupied country. But on 29 August 1943, the situation changed drastically.

Denmark now became a country at war, and the conflict significantly intensified. The Jews in Denmark began to fear for their lives. A month later, the order from Germany came to deport Denmark's 7,000 Jews to concentration camps. But by then most of the Jewish population had been warned.

Most Jews were evacuated starting in September 2023. It cost between DKK 1,000 and 5,000 per person and took place by fishing boats. The economically conscious Jacobsen found that price too high. He therefore bought a rowing boat and shared the cost with his travel companions – his girlfriend Jonna, elite rower Herbert Marcus, and free speech activist Poul Henningsen and his wife Inger. Poul Henningsen was not in danger because of his race, but because of his work as a poet and social critic.

It was not the first time that Jacobsen had felt the effects of Nazi Germany breathing down his neck. In the first year of the occupation, both he and Poul Henningsen had gone underground due to communist persecution. Jacobsen managed to wriggle out of it by maintaining that he was not a communist, but had only been interested in the Soviet Union for architectural reasons. His amateur film reel from Moscow was presented as justification and evidence. That said, for a while now Jacobsen had been preparing as much as possible for a tightening of measures from

Germany. His two sons had been baptised as Christians. He had sought to downplay his Jewish roots.

Crossing the Øresund in an ordinary dinghy or rowboat with a low freeboard was a daring and dangerous, but late in the evening of 30 September, they succeeded. The professional rower Herbert Marcus got the boat out into the open sea. For four hours they struggled across the Øre-sund Strait on the 15-kilometre journey, while scooping out encroaching water and anxiously scouting for German patrol boats. Would they be captured by the Germans? They would have been easy prey.

The boat landed at Landskrona. Wet and exhausted, they pulled it ashore and headed inland. A glass factory was their first encounter with Sweden. The next morning they reported to Landskrona town hall, ironically a building that Jacobsen would later redesign.

Jacobsen was well received in Stockholm. Influential and admiring colleagues including Alvar Aalto and Sven Markelius welcomed him and his travel companion Poul Henningsen at the same apartment complex in the middle of Stockholm. Far from all the Danish refugees were able to travel as freely as Poul Henningsen and Arne Jacobsen. If you couldn't support yourself, you were interned in a refugee camp. Their travel companion Herbert Marcus signed up for military service in the Danish Brigade.

Jacobsen was given a good job at HSB, the Swedish Tenants' Savings and Building Society. From the outset, this pioneering architectural firm contributed to the development of the welfare state through the Swedish political concept of "The People's Home." It was a firm that Sven Markelius had previously worked for, and for which he had helped define the professional profile. Among other things, he had designed the *Collective House* apartment building in 1935, the purpose of which was to integrate women into the labour market, by having people employed by the building who would take over the daily running of the home. There was a restaurant at the bottom of the building, and from here a dumb waiter would bring the dish of the day up to each apartment.

For one month, the hardworking Jacobsen worked as an architect at HSB. Then he put down his pencil and spent the rest of the war pursuing his interest and dream – botany. The man who had once designed town halls, theatres, villa after villa, apartment buildings, factories, furniture, and lamps, now put all of this on the back-burner. Had he grown tired of architecture, which had been such a strong driving force for him, or did he simply want to spend more time with his future wife?

One thing is certain, their time in Sweden led to a close partnership between him and Jonna, also professionally. It was Jonna's training as a cotton printer that inspired them to create the large collection of textile patterns that they designed together for Nordiska Kompaniet.

Jacobsen had a consistently steady hand and over time produced many watercolour perspectives of his house projects. No effect was spared. Like another marine painter who deftly painted ships with billowing sails, backlit against a threatening horizon and illuminated by the sea spray, Jacobsen was also well aware of how to put his project in the spotlight. Most often, his drawings were bold and humorous, supplemented with opaque colours and gouache. These were utilitarian watercolours, with the aim of selling yet another project.

Although he also drew many sketches and watercolours of nature and culture throughout his life, they remained tucked away. The watercolours were rarely shown at exhibitions, but in 1954 Jacobsen was asked on the radio about an exhibited watercolour of Greek ruins at Aarhus City Hall. It is through his project drawings and watercolours that we see the real Jacobsen, with no filter – a most talented advertising illustrator.

The architect spent the next year and a half learning his wife's craft, namely textile design. A space for freedom, inspiration, and reciprocity evolved between them. However, he stuck close to his own field, because it was design drawings that were needed in the situation. The work process seems to have been as follows: Initial studies outside in the real environment. Careful but quick drawings on watercolour paper stretched on an easel. Then home for further drawing and pattern composition. And then to complete the puzzle of filling in the fields for a harmonious whole

without any clashing sections. To start off with, these compositions could also be made by cutting out drawings and photos.

Should the fabric be organza, chintz, or linen? Different textile types would reproduce the print differently. Translucent or illuminated – how would the colours change? But what about the pleats in a curtain? Or perhaps the pattern would hug a body like dress fabric? There was plenty for the Jacobsen couple to decide on. The textiles should be versatile – how many different colour combinations should there be? Some motifs such as Bamboo and Anemone were very adaptable, while Forest Floor could handle only a few changes. Could the motif be transferred to wallpaper? This would provide extra income, they thought.

The motifs became more and more demanding along the way. They went from the relatively simple block prints that did not require much of a gripper margin, to the more demanding repro film prints with super-fine adjustments and many colour combinations. Jonna zealously monitored the quality and colours of the production, necessitating numerous train journeys back and forth to the printing house in Floda, between Borås and Gothenburg, which was quite a way from Stockholm. She did this right up until the grand premiere at Nordiska Kompaniet in the autumn of 1944.

It was not a small collection – on the contrary, in fact, and at least 15 patterns were created. We can sense that this was a big investment on the part of Nordiska Kompaniet. It was not just a sales exhibition. Artistically, the exhibition

Vegetation for Nordiska Kompaniet, 1944. Textiles often have a white or black background colour so that the motif stands out more clearly. Here we can sense how the white can be perceived as snow, through which the spring vegetation emerges during the thaw.

The textile *Trapez*, which was probably produced by Grautex in 1951. Jacobsen worked in different

directions with his motif cycles relating to textiles.

Most common were the geometric types seen here, and the beds of wildflowers, where you get

the sense that he just sat down and painted what was in front of him.

←*Reed* for Textil Lassen, 1948. Reeds and bamboo are perfect for painting with a watercolour brush, something that Japanese visual art makes abundant use of.

Jacobsen followed suit with his brush strokes. This is a rather complicated textile, using seven different printing frames.

Anemone for Nordiska Kompaniet, 1944. Later produced by Textil Lassen, Almedahl, and Designletters. Three printing frames with different colour sets

in blue, green, grey, and black. Here the perspective is a little different as we look directly down into the grass and see the little harbingers of spring.

was also given the green light when Sweden's National Museum, which houses the Swedish Museum of Applied Arts, purchased most of the textiles for their collection.

The textiles were displayed in many different guises – not only as curtains, but also as dresses, scarves, furniture covers, and even parasols and canopies. The motifs emanated from everything that the war had destroyed and that people longed for. We are a long way from functionalism and white walls. That ideology was replaced by a romantic longing for respite. There was a need for recreation during these terrible years. Nature couldn't get close enough. It was brought right into people's living rooms with a large paintbrush on canvas, translucent floral curtains in front of the windows, furniture covers – and what about anemones on the wallpaper throughout the living room?

They succeeded. Once again, Jacobsen had foreseen and developed a new trend to perfection. He designed very few houses while in exile. A summer house and a competition for stock house designs, the latter together

with good friend Nils Koppel. Here too, the projects had a clear connection with nature. Most interestingly, it was in Sweden that he began designing his own house, which was already intended as a terraced house. It appears that the land at Klampenborg had already been acquired or at least designated during the occupation.

The sketches for the houses also testified to a new beginning or a change in style with buildings that have a repetitive pattern, inside and out. Quite like the repeats in his and Jonna's textiles. It is easy to believe that his own house grew out of his work with textiles. This insight into the adaptation of the print and the repetition of the motif became a guiding principle for him in his architecture in the years to come. It became very visible in the design elements. Few chairs were modelled like Jacobsen's in clear graphic forms that could not only withstand repetition, like soldiers in formation, but became quite beautiful when they were arranged, angled, and bent towards each other around a table, much like a curtain.

The war put a severe damper on construction, in particular due to a shortage of materials, and this naturally was quick to affect the activities of the design studios. Jacobsen had his two projects to finish – Aarhus City Hall and Søllerød Town Hall – and there were also a few family homes to be designed, as well as a couple of larger residential developments. But then the commissions started to dry up somewhat, compared to the pre-war years. Larger public-sector buildings and other civil engineering commissions were virtually non-existent in these years.

This pattern was called *Mushrooms* and produced by Grautex, before later being named *Arne*. It was printed as wallpaper at Boråstapeter with two printing frames. A simple geometric pattern with finely co-ordinated bluish and reddish-brown shades. With its subdued effect, it was suitable for drapery, which the Jacobsen couple paid close attention to.

Little happened on the design front either, because there was no money for new furnishings by way of furniture and lamps, or materials to produce them for that matter. Arne's marriage to Marie was on its last legs, and while working on Søllerød Town Hall he met the textile printer, Jonna Møller, with whom he struck up a good friendship. They worked well together. Before long, they became lovers and got engaged. Before the situation escalated in Denmark's relationship with its Nazi occupiers, and Arne Jacobsen and Jonna Møller had to flee to Sweden, they managed to design some textiles and wallpapers with leaf motifs, which were shown at the Artists' Spring Exhibition in 1943.

However, it was only after they arrived in Stockholm in the autumn of 1943 that the couple's development of new textiles really took off, based on Arne's brushstrokes and Jonna's insight into textile printing techniques. Something new was brewing in Jacobsen's career; sparked by exile, his relationship with Jonna Møller, and his encounter with the textile printing methods. The architect spent the next year and a half learning his wife's craft – textile design. A space for freedom, inspiration, and reciprocity evolved between them.

However, one would think that cotton printing was an old technique, ever evolving throughout the 20th century based on age-old methods, just like earthenware manufacturing or silversmithing. It had existed for hundreds of years, so it should have been common knowledge. But that wasn't the case. In fact, the technique was revived in the 1930s as a new element in applied arts. First as block prints, cut blocks of wood or linoleum, and later developed through photo-technical processes with repro film, which allowed for multiple colours and complicated overlays.

In the mid-1930s, cotton printing was revived in Sweden thanks to, among others, the exiled Austrian architect Josef Frank as the frontman of Svenskt Tenn which, in addition to pewter goods, produced all kinds of interior design objects with furniture and lighting in an elegant Art Deco style. Around the same time, Marie Gudme Leth established an art printing house in Denmark. It was here that Jonna Møller trained as an apprentice.

Oak leaves AJJ from
1944 was included in the
exhibition at Nordiska
Kompaniet. Arne and
Jonna Jacobsen worked
a lot with drapery. Here,
the vertical tendrils fade
a little and seem to have
fewer oak leaves when
the curtain is drawn. Look
at Albert Naur's version
from Aarhus City Hall
of a leaf vine on pages
48-49, which Jacobsen was
inspired by.

An important player in Scandinavia was the large Swedish department store, Nordiska Kompaniet, established in 1902. It was an institution that, with its style and spirit, reached far beyond Sweden's borders and collaborated with international department stores. From the outset, an important part of the company's business strategy was the design of furniture, textiles, and other interior design elements. The Danish architect Svend Thoresen was hired in 1925 to handle interior design and exhibition tasks, and in 1927 the sculptor and architect Axel Einar Hjorth was hired as chief architect.

The principal intention was for Nordiska Kompaniet to make a mark at international exhibitions with Swedish names. The style quickly went from imitation baroque and renaissance to more contemporary expressions in art deco and functionalism, but still handmade. Furniture was exhibited at the World Exhibition of 1929 in Barcelona and the domestic Stockholm Exhibition in 1930. Several well-known Swedish architects were hired to come up with their ideas for a contemporary interior design – Carl Malmsten, Sigurd Lewerentz, and Sven Markelius. All produced unique furnishings for Gunnar Asplund's Stockholm exhibition. It wasn't until the mid-1930s that Nordiska Kompaniet switched to mass-produced furniture with collections of bold pine furniture intended for Stockholmers who now had enough free time and money for a holiday home. They were designed by Axel Einar Hjorth.

Block print from before
the crossing to Sweden
in the autumn of 1943,
with the wreath motif
used at Søllerød Town
Hall. Here it is combined
to make a charming
table arrangement with
shaker chairs reminiscent
of those that Jacobsen
designed for Novo.

Meanwhile in the early 1930s, the Swedish textile designer Astrid Sampe returned home to Sweden fresh from the Royal College of Art in London. She was a co-exhibitor at the Swedish pavilion at the World's Fair in New York in 1939 and had become responsible for the textile department at Nordiska Kompaniet, which had allied itself with Erik Ljungberg Tekstiltrykkeri in Floda. The ubiquitous Sven Markelius had designed the Swedish pavilion in New York, and over in the Finnish pavilion Alvar Aalto had made a splash with the staging. "Scandinavian Modern" had come into vogue, albeit with different expressions. "Swedish Modern", which a British critic called "Swedish Grace", was more decorative and "floral" than the more pared back Finnish style.

Into this international environment with textile printers Astrid Sampe and architect Sven Markelius came Jonna and Arne Jacobsen. As mentioned before, some of Jacobsen's first textile patterns were designed in Denmark.

After Arne Jacbosen fled to Sweden, Poul Erik Skriver, the only remaining employee at the design studio, sent the textile designs to Stockholm via Magasin du Nord, where they could be printed. The motifs from Søllerød Town Hall were then used in Sweden as curtain fabrics, as well as for pillowcases, placemats, and even a tea cosy.

All of Jacobsen's sketches for textile patterns are undated, so we can only guess in what order they were created. That said, the curtain for the wedding room at Søllerød Town Hall must be one of the first. A completed wreath of green fern leaves on a grey linen curtain, simple and stylised. A subsequent motif might then be *Autumn Leaves*, which is in a way very architectural. In addition to the motif with its simple and stylised fallen leaves, there are also various effects. From tightly packed foliage when the curtain is open, to leaves falling from the tree when drawn.

Vine or *Quaking Grass*.
Three printing frames in
green or grey have been
used here. Produced by
Cotil in 1955 and later
transferred to Georg
Jensen Damask. The love
for individual plant types
can be seen throughout
Jacobsen's production.
Simple plant species are
honestly and meticulously
embraced, not as a sober
documentation, but as
a play with composition,
which lends itself to the
meandering possibilities
of textile.

Ferns was probably
produced as a block print
for Magasin du Nord in
the early 1940s and taken
to Sweden and Nordiska
Kompaniet.

Drawing as a livelihood

Although Jacobsen drew many sketches and watercolours of nature and culture throughout his life, they were hidden away in folders and rolls in the archive, and this is where we find them today. At the Danish Art Library, there are some motif sketches in the very large collection of Jacobsen's drawings, and they are more careful and neat than those he is best known for. With the finest of brushes, he painted motifs for Swedish placemats of horses grazing in a field. He has carefully drawn flowering meadows, streams, and horses bathing in a lake. But the incarnate architect couldn't help himself: The fences and horse pens are circular with carefully composed, asymmetrical trees.

Wide brushes, thin brushes, fast swipes, and slow strokes. Colours that flow into each other, wet into wet, or are framed with a thin contour line in the best cartoon style. Jacobsen makes genius use of countless methods.

← Christmas pattern made as a bookmark, probably from Christmas 1943, beautifully produced using the thinnest of brush strokes. A quite unusual watercolour by Jacobsen.

↓ A group of Arabian horses, presumably from the winter of 1943/44. A humorous watercolour and maybe just an inspiration for a pattern.

As we can see in some of the later sketches, Jacobsen is letting loose here, only to tighten up the motif later when the final pattern was to be composed.

→→ This is a so-called cardboard pattern for *Lupins*. In this case, it is the basis for a wallpaper, painted in opaque colours on pieces of cardboard. There are seven different colours that are placed together in pairs, like light and shadow.

It is also a puzzle – the cardboard is divided into four pieces to enable Arne and Jonna Jacobsen to work on how the pattern shifts and repeats itself down the fabric or wallpaper.

Perhaps these were the first motifs from the couple's time in Stockholm? If so, they would have been designed in Arne and Jonna's modest apartment. With the meditative Christmas motifs, we get a sense that things have calmed down. Ideas are starting to fall into place, and in 1943, three days before Christmas Eve, Arne and Jonna get married. 1944, on the other hand, was ushered in with the news that the Danish poet-priest Kaj Munk had been exterminated by the Gestapo on 4 January. A universal feeling of helplessness in the face of brutality was a cruel wake-up call. Especially for Poul Henningsen, because he knew that there had also been a bullet with his name on it. It was time for New Year's letters. Poul Henningsen wrote to his ex-wife: "There are great joys and great sorrows". Arne dropped a bombshell on his ex-wife Marie, writing that he had married Jonna, but that the children should not suffer any financial hardship. Instead Jonna had painfully given up custody of her two children to their father. A lonely Christmas.

↓ *Docks*. Another of Jacobsen's centrepieces, where he works with a central group of plants that weave in and out of each other.

↑ *Crown Imperial* for Nordiska Kompaniet 1944, later Lunggreen and most recently Boråstapeter. This is probably one of the best-known of Jacobsen's early motifs. The motifs surrounding *Springtime Collection* were about the coming liberation. Motifs like *Chain*, *Yes-No*, *Daisies* (where you pull off the leaves: he loves me, he loves me not). And finally the proud *Crown Imperial* – the flower that was punished in the Garden of Eden when its leaves arrogantly reached toward the sky. God decreed that it should be punished by having its flower head point downwards.

→ The template for *Lupins* is meticulously drawn in pencil and later painted over in imaginative colours, whereas the final cardboard pattern uses powerful strokes, as seen on the previous spread.

The new year, now upon them, they had a grand plan to depict nature through the emergence of spring. The small pointed brushes were replaced with larger and wider ones. They put winter behind them and sought to forget the war for a while. The possibility of peace was edging closer and the fortunes of the war were on the side of the Allies. The enterprising stems of the plants channelled their way up through the frozen and barren soil. There was no shortage of clichés. We can well imagine how the initial marketing meeting at Nordiska Kompaniet was overflowing with them. *Springtime Collection* was a tribute to nature and destined to be a commercial success.

↓ *Wildflower Bouquet* for Textil Lassen. A classic textile motif is, of course, the bouquet. *Wildflower Bouquet* and *Larkspurs* are Jacobsen's offering, most likely inspired by Albert Naur's giant bouquets painted on the wall in the wedding hall at Aarhus City Hall. See pages 48-49.

↑ The future Swedish royal couple Queen Louise and King Gustav VI Adolf with Jacobsen somewhat discreetly in the background.

→ *Chain* for Nordiska Kompaniet, 1944. In this staging, *Chain* is used as the fabric for clothing, furniture, and the parasol. The Danish and Swedish flags placed in a pile of sand complete the story of the relationship between the two countries that cannot be stopped by shackles or chains.

↓ *Meadow* for Nordiska Kompaniet, 1944. The dress on the mannequin clearly demonstrates how the motif is still legible despite its folds.

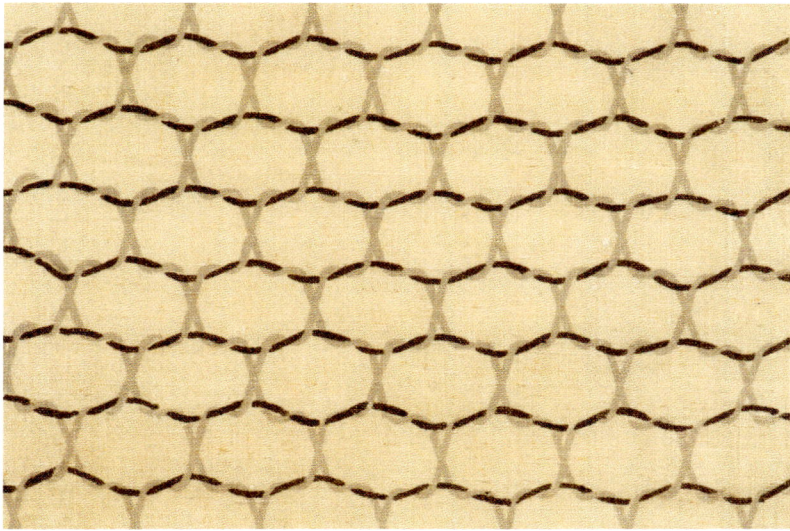

← Waves for Nordiska Kompaniet, 1944. So modern that even the American design company KNOLL produced it under license.

↑ Chain for Nordiska Kompaniet, 1944. Geometric patterns were a regular motif group for Jacobsen and became a predominant theme in his later years. We can see how the motifs are repeated and reformulated. *Chain* become the humorous *Net* a few years later.

↓ Forest Floor for Nordiska Kompaniet, 1944, later taken over by Tapettrykkeriet. One of the heavier motifs from Jacobsen's hand, but quite suitable for upholstery fabric. Here, the textile is stiffer and stretched out so that the motif stands out clearly. This requires it to be carefully placed on upholstered furniture.

Jacobsen began with snowdrops, anemones, and crown imperials. He used classic backgrounds with areas that were either white or completely dark. He painted the meadow in bloom and the ditch edge by the road, the city park with benches and people, and a rather gloomy pond with drifting water plants. A forest floor with a rotten stump. A dock leaf and informal bouquets of autumn flowers and larkspurs. But there were also the more abstract patterns resembling interconnected wire mesh, called *Chain* (war may also have been used as a motif), and then there were *Yes-No* and *Bio-Bio*.

Bamboo became a real favourite among painters. With the right flick of the brush, it was almost impossible to not produce bamboo leaves. So Japanese, in a non-Japanese way. Something was produced for every taste and budget. There were affordable options with few colours and minimal customisation, and then there were the expensive and complicated options with many colours. Multiple versions and qualities of fabric were produced, both for furniture and curtains, as well as for dresses and scarves. In some cases, the patterns were also transferred to wallpapers.

The modern Arne Jacobsen took shape in Stockholm, but how and why? He was inspired by many things. At first glance, it seems natural that textiles have given him new content. After all, textiles didn't just occupy him during his exile in Sweden, and he continued working with them over the next 25 years and the rest of his hectic working life. He drew and produced more than 150 patterns, all in collaboration with Jonna Jacobsen – a business model that would prove to keep his architectural studio afloat for several years after Germany's occupation and his return to a building-less Denmark.

Botany gave him freedom to explore and a foundation of an expression that would later emerge in the form of design and buildings.

Over time, the patterns became more and more abstract, not least to suit the spirit of the times. Consequently, we can see how his drawing technique changes from watercolour brushes in the 1940s to torn graph paper, photocopies, and finally professional fabric pens in the 1950s. On the commercial side, he learnt to create and orchestrate a large collection for a mass market. In terms of design, he turned away from the site-specific designs and his own construction projects which had been his focus before the war. He now designed products that were not only used in his own houses, but also in the homes and offices of completely anonymous consumers all over the world.

↓ Headscarves. The idea is to show how beautifully the different patterns drape gracefully around a woman's head.

→ The happy designer lies in a flower meadow and draws one of his favourite motifs. Advertisement from the American

Cyrus Clark's collection *Printemps Prints*. As an advertisement in *House & Garden*, it is targeted at new fresh

tones in the home, but you can read the superlatives in the ad text for yourself.

decorate with springtime magic

Cyrus Clark's
printemps prints

for every room in your house . . .

utterly refreshing, completely different in design and color. The artist has used a new perspective. Right in the midst of flowering fields, lush spring meadows and the forest ground, he has painted these subjects as he saw them at ground level. Printemps Prints have captured the gaiety and abandon of a perfect spring for your home. They are right for modern interiors, wholly charming for 18th century or traditional rooms. At leading stores.

"Tulips"
50 inch Everglaze*
Chintz and 50 inch
Cotton

"Branches"
36 inch Everglaze*
Chintz

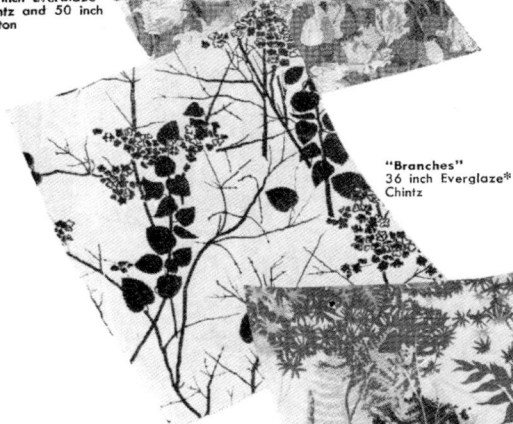

"Forest Ground"
50 inch Hand
Printed Cotton

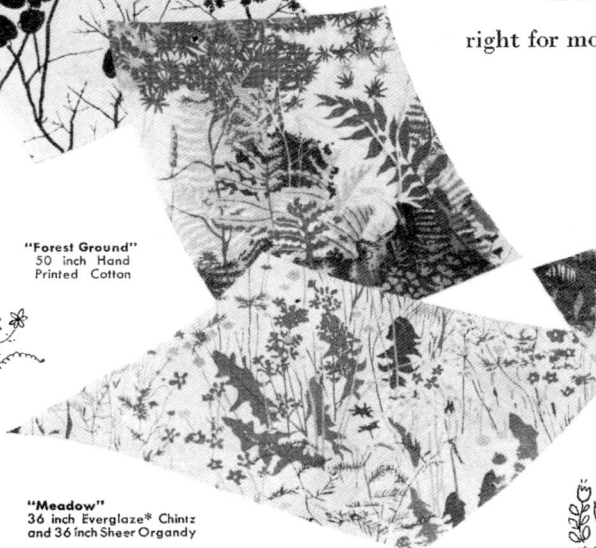

"Crown Imperial"
50 inch everglaze* Chintz

"Meadow"
36 inch Everglaze* Chintz
and 36 inch Sheer Organdy

*®—Trade Mark J. B. & S. Co.

Hyacinths for Textil Lassen, 1948. Jacobsen plays around with a graphic style here, with those plants that have sprouted and those still wearing their dunce hat. The textile patterns *Hyacinths*, *Net* (with lemons), *Cloche*, and *Tulips* were Arne and Jonna's new, more light-hearted designs after the war. Large colourful motifs that brightened up the living room and could be seen from far down the road, letting neighbours know that you were on trend and ready for the post-war boom.

With *Springtime Collection*, Jacobsen was no longer a locally minded architect rooted in the artisanal community in Gentofte and the surrounding area. He was now having fruitful discussions with companies selling his work to an emerging global market.

By the end of the war in 1945, his textiles were being exhibited in New York at the Lord & Taylor department store on Fifth Avenue. That it was here shouldn't come as a surprise. Their new CEO Dorothy Shaver, also called "The First Lady of Retailing", had just taken up the role and had her finger truly on the pulse. If it anyone could be credited, it was she who created the modern department store with the customer at the centre. She was also a co-founder of the American fashion industry.

Back in Copenhagen in 1948, Jacobsen had a solo exhibition at the Danish Museum of Art and Design, where he showcased what he was working on internationally. As he told the press: "There are the textiles I like and the ones people want". For the Danish company Grautex, he had designed new textiles with cosy, homely patterns such as *Cloche*, *Hyacinths*, and *Tulips*, as well as *Aircraft* for the boys' room, dancing across motorways. With all this under his belt, a few years later he was able to embark on what would make him internationally famous: Jacobsen's modern furniture.

The most important thing he took home from Stockholm was the human aspect. The memory of the soulmate who died a few years earlier, Gunnar Asplund, whom he admired and was inspired by, collaborator Sven Markelius, and not least his second wife Jonna, who was to be of such great importance to him in everything, not least in the professional sphere. Gunnar Asplund was probably more of a formal connection with whom he had many a good conversation about architecture. Jacobsen admired his architecture as seen in the Stockholm Public Library, Gothenburg Town Hall, and his extensive work on Skogskyrkegården cemetery, which was completed together with Sigurd Lewerentz. Jacobsen drew direct inspiration from Asplund when he designed his summer house in the same style and used style elements from Asplund's town hall in his own.

Gunnar Asplund and Sven Markelius were 16 and 12 years older than Arne, respectively, so they were a generation and a lot of life experience ahead of him. Markelius was a functionalist to the core and co-published the manifesto "Acceptera" together with Asplund and the historian and chair of the Swedish Crafts Association Gregor Paulsson, among others. The manifesto was created as a continuation of the Stockholm Exhibition in 1930 and forms part of the material and visual background for the Swedish concept of "The People's Home", which formed the basis for the welfare state ideology in Sweden and the other Scandinavian countries. Markelius subsequently designed the *Collective House* in Stockholm, in which he himself lived for the next 30 years, and took special care of as an unofficial caretaker. Meanwhile, he was associated with Nordiska Kompaniet as a commercial designer.

It has been said that Jonna had some control over Jacobsen, and was even able to put him on a diet. She had a keen eye for aesthetics and its possibilities. Over the years, it's possible that she became just as experienced a designer, and perhaps also with the same talent for building architecture as

textile design, which she originally trained in. Although this was probably somewhat behind the scenes. It's likely that she had the same role as the architect wives Lilly Reich, Charlotte Periand, and Ray Eames. All three were vital collaborators and fellow students of great architects during their most prolific professional periods. As a textile designer, Lilly Reich had a strong influence on Ludwig Mies van der Rohe's furniture and draperies for the German pavilion at the 1929 Barcelona World Exhibition and his "Samt und Seide" exhibition in Cologne in 1927. She worked alongside him at the Bauhaus. But when Mies van der Rohe went to the US, she stayed in Germany. After that, no more furniture was developed by Mies van der Rohe. It was the same when Charlotte Periand left Le Corbusier. His source of new furniture and designs dried up. And Ray Eames was Charles Eames's visual eye. Together they created countless pieces of furniture, films, and exhibitions, although it was often only his name that was written under the chair seats, until she was finally honoured around 20 years ago and now appears in the brand with her husband: Designed by Ray and Charles Eames.

In the same way, Jonna and Arne can be seen as business partners with a newly developed third branch of the architectural and design business. They followed Alvar and Aino Aalto's division of work in their design studio. Alvar took care of construction. Aino was responsible for building the organisation around Artek, their jointly owned furniture company from 1935, which they shared with Maire Gullichsen and Nils-Gustav Hahl. The Aaltos's business idea was clear – to produce in-house designed furniture and glass that could be used in the many houses that the couple was responsible for. This meant that the design studio not only received royalties on the design, but also profited from the manufacture of the products. Arne and Jonna chose the simpler and freer approach – working with independent manufacturers they trusted and who could produce what would become major design collections, and where their return was the royalties.

Lemons in Net for Textil Lassen are the obvious motif in front of a kitchen window. The movement of lemons dropping into the net when the curtain is pulled aside is quite witty.

Back to work

In June 1945, after 20 months in exile, Arne and Jonna Jacobsen returned to Arne's small and now no longer very profitable design studio. At that time it was located in a red end-of-terrace house on Ørnegårdsvej in Gentofte. Originally designed for Novo Industries, but now leased to the architect himself. Three desks in the basement for the employees and a small private room with a high window for the boss. The paintbrush was replaced with the telephone – it was time to get the architectural drawing room working again. Mayors and master builders were on the receiving end of several of phone calls from Jacobsen, who believed that it was schools that needed special attention.

A large villa in Odense for a tinplate manufacturer and a school in the Faroe Islands, probably obtained through connections to his Faroese ex-wife Marie and her sister Estrid, were on the cards. The school was a visually strong project with a gymnasium made of multi-coloured boulders, situated dramatically overlooking a river and field of grass. It never came about, and the project is now sadly lost. His former consortium of tradespeople also had apartment blocks under construction. That was all – not much compared to the construction activity of earlier times.

By a twist of fate, many of Jacobsen's houses are concentrated at Jægersborg, and some of his buildings wind in and out of the motorway network here – including his own house that was almost demolished to make way for it. It is a typical 'war house' filled with chimneys and small rooms, intended for heating with a tiled stove and peat.

For seven years, from 1943 to 1950, Jacobsen built very few buildings, and he almost resorted to dusting off unfinished projects from before the war. The Ibstrupparken II apartment blocks, the youth housing at Jægersborg, and some terraced houses in the same location, which were a continuation of the ones he himself lived in at Hørsholmvejen. DKK 700 for each house built wasn't much compared to the DKK 500 from a proposed textile pattern, especially considering that came with a royalty cheque. His advice to his stepson Peter, who wanted to be an architect, was: "Forget it – it's a dead-end job!" But Arne, who now had a good side income from his mass-produced textiles, was confident. He could afford to invest in and rebuild his architectural practice.

War cast a long shadow, also for architects, although there were glimmers of hope. Europe had to be rebuilt. In many countries, bulldozers and trucks worked to remove the enormous piles of rubble – many cities simply had to be taken to landfill and rebuilt. Denmark, on the other hand, was mostly intact with only a few buildings that had been bombed. Nexø was the exception, which was largely destroyed after Soviet bombing raids. Esbjerg and Vejle suffered minor damage, while the Shell building and the French School in Copenhagen had been destroyed by British bombs.

Added to that was a huge influx of refugees. Around 260,000 refugees had come to the country from East Prussia due to the advance of Soviet forces there. This put pressure on schools and other facilities, which now had to accommodate this influx of people, which constituted more than 5% of the Danish population. It would be several years before they could return home to a changed Germany. In addition, there were 17,000 Danes who returned home from Sweden, including the interim army: the Danish Brigade. In addition, there were general shortages of goods and rationing of all necessities.

The telephone alone was not enough to get commissions. He had to get out his paintbrush again and put his popular watercolours to work. Jacobsen was an experienced competitive architect, and many of his buildings throughout his 40-year career were won by way of open competitions and subsequently built. He took part in more than 100 competitions during his life. After the war, he threw himself into the small number of architectural competitions that popped up. He took part in 11 competitions from the end of the war to 1950, which resulted in three first prizes, one second prize, two third prizes, and four commendations. This brought in fees, of course, but not enough to create a meaningful revenue for an architectural design studio. It must have been a frustrating few years with a lot of waiting to see whether a project would come to pass. None of the competitions that Jacobsen won during this period went on to be built, and they were initially small commissions. Had they been built, we would have seen a forest pavilion in Hobro, a memorial, and a gunnery house with port facilities. However, two of the competitions led Arne to a field of work for which he would later become known – municipal schools.

Clover for Nordiska Kompaniet, 1944. Another symphony of colour that illustrates the joy of sitting on the edge of a ditch.

KLÖVER ARNE JACOBSEN COLLECTION almedahls 1983

For a young, newly qualified architect of 25 years old with hopes of stardom, it must of course have been a dream to be employed at Jacobsen's design studio, and then to work alone on the conceptual level, working on competitions most of the time. "It was my job to familiarise myself with the competition schedule and produce the initial sketches, Jacobsen did not interfere in this," recalls Henrik Iversen. Awaiting him the next morning, there were typically amendments and sketches from the master himself, made with a soft pencil. These then had to be translated into more concrete drawings. The tone of the studio was straightforward and liberal. Swearing and cursing were commonplace.

Henrik Iversen was hired at the same time as a third person in the design studio. Jacobsen complained about the high salary of DKK 400 per month, while Henrik Iversen complained about the low salary of DKK 400. At other design studios, they earnt more. But in addition to being generally cautious, it must be pointed out that Jacobsen had just returned home from exile and wasn't exactly flush with money.

Henrik Iversen got close to his patriarchal boss. Too close, he thought at times. In his eagerness to work, he had ignored the warning from former employees when he rented the townhouse at the other end of the development, just a minute's walk from his boss's domain. After all, Jacobsen did not believe that a wife and small children should prevent employees from doing their work. But who moved in where is debatable. Mrs. Iversen also came to work at the design studio as a secretary. It was the same marital distribution as before, like when Hans and Inga Wegner worked for Jacobsen and Møller on Aarhus City Hall.

Once Henrik Iversen had done the preliminary work and drawn a number of sketches, the actual work came with the competition. In the design studio, everyone was now working towards the deadline, and the intensity increased considerably. This was Jacobsen's work in a nutshell throughout his more than 40 active years. Always with the same division of labour – the employees read the schedule and held the pencils, while Arne oriented himself on the building site and then slowly entered the competition through conversations with his employees. And then the 'advertising artist' came into play. One could say that Jacobsen only completed the project once his suggestive watercolours were completed on the same evening that the competition project was due to be delivered to the post office.

They worked seven days in the last week before handover, and then without sleeping for the last day and a half, their eyes held open by matchsticks – the employees had to take amphetamines to get them through it. Everyone was busy. Basic perspectives were drawn, constructed, pasted, and finally produced, which the 'advertising artist' in the adjacent room could use to produce the signature watercolour that would ultimately win the competition. The watercolour could be viewed as it was dried on the tiled stove. Jacobsen used every means at his disposal when applying the final brushstrokes. The employees' coffee cups were good for dipping his brush in and also for extinguishing his cigar. The clock ticking, the last chance for submission was 23:00 sharp at the Central Station post office.

Jonna could almost feel the nervousness downstairs and came down to help with gluing the cardboard. Meanwhile, Arne went to get his BMW sports sedan warmed up. It was his much-loved car from before the war, which had been hidden away in a barn far out in the countryside during the Nazi occupation – it still smelled of wet hay and chickens.

With absolutely no time to spare, at 22:35, Arne put the pedal to the metal and sped towards the Central Station post office some ten kilometres away.

The staff were given half a day off the next day and showed up at lunchtime to a cold design studio – the tiled stove had gone out. Jacobsen greeted them grumpily, puffing on his American cigarette: "You can't run a bloody design studio when your employees have to go and have a lie down every time they've drawn a few lines." Handing out bonuses to the hard-working people who worked on the competition was out of the question. Four hours of work had already been wasted that morning. The deliciously fragrant cigarette was stubbed out in the ashtray with the assurance "And this tastes like crap, too." Construction drawings for terraced houses and apartment blocks were brought out again – a new day could begin, albeit half asleep.

Unique and industrial

The Cabinetmakers' Guild's exhibition in the autumn of 1949 was one of the best of the 40 annual exhibitions that it had ever arranged between 1927 and 1966. This Copenhagen event made the newspaper headlines every year, but this year in particular was something of a watershed. Visitors could see the furniture that would later be counted among the great furniture classics of Danish design. These included the *Chieftain Chair* by Finn Juhl and Hans Wegner's armchair, which he himself called *The Round Chair*, but which a US design magazine later simply called *The Chair* due to its sheer simplicity – there was no other chair so beautiful and solid. Since these were initially prototypes made specifically for this exhibition, the reviewers and spectators could only sigh longingly, and ask expectantly when production would start.

The professionals could only surmise that they had some future classics on their hands here. Furniture that would set such a high bar that, even more than 70 years later, it is still in production as a sought-after modern design. What was once produced in very small numbers by joiners was now produced by machines, at least partially. Master carpenters,

members of the guild, and residents of the Copenhagen area entered into a pact with furniture designers in 1930 to steer the craft of fine joinery and upholstery in a more modern and marketable direction by way of exhibitions and competitions. Consequently, an increasingly superior aesthetic dialogue emerged between the architects and the approximately 500 members of the guild over the years. However, their collaboration was mostly focused on the development of wooden furniture. This excluded functional furniture, which consisted predominantly of metal structures. Blacksmiths had their own guild, and it was generally understood not to interfere with them.

This tradition was nothing new. Architects and master carpenters had worked together for centuries, initially for the nobility and royalty, where architects such as Harsdoff and C.F. Hansen designed everything from the castle buildings themselves to their interiors. At the beginning of the 20th century, private homes and public buildings were also furnished with the fine craftsmanship of master carpenters.

From the exhibition at Nordiska Kompaniet in Stockholm. The leading Nordic department store at the time, with space for displaying large collections.

And these craftspeople often mastered several styles of their own accord, which they were trained in during their apprenticeships and later by copying from pattern books, especially those from the English Chippendale and Sheraton. Customers could browse the books and choose a model that appealed to them, and then it was the skill of the cabinetmaker that determined how closely the result resembled the original. If you were a privileged citizen in a provincial town, you went to the local carpenter, whose skill and experience would build a complete dining room set with six chairs, a table with extendable leaves, and an accompanying sideboard. If you wanted your walls panelled, this could also be done in mahogany or in stained beech as a cheaper option. If they were really pushing the boat out, the customer would order a set of drawings from an architect, pay them for their time, and then go to the master carpenter.

In other words, furniture was designed and produced as one-offs. When the architect received a new commission, they started a new page, designed a new furniture series, and were paid for it. Series production was never really an option. However, in some cases, there were small series of upholstered furniture. This is how Jacobsen worked with Rud. Rasmussen and Littmann, whereas Viggo Boesen and Flemming Lassen drew for the Carpenters' Guild's alderman A.J. Iversen. In this way, the architects' upholstered furniture was produced in quantities of up to 50 pieces, and they were perhaps then remunerated by way of an amount per piece.These were small series that could be full of variations, because the buyer still had a say. Should the back be a little higher? Should it have slightly shorter legs? What length should the sofa be? Everything was possible, and it also depended on the craftsperson in question as to how the details would turn out.

The guild exhibitions were based on annual themes such as 'A three-room apartment for a working-class family', 'The young couple', or 'A penthouse for a young businesswoman'. The exhibitors would then design their stands around these themes. It was then up to the architect/carpenter partnership to design and produce all the furniture for the exhibition home in question before the deadline. The collaboration between Finn Juhl and master carpenter Niels Vodder involved developing the finest details that could possibly be produced to stand out from the competitors at neighbouring stands. This one annual exhibition was a big show intended to spawn commissions for the rest of the year.

But there was an unfortunate circumstance back in 1949 that resulted in the end of the Cabinetmakers' Guild's exhibitions some

20 years later in 1966. The problem was what could best be called 'development'. The hourly wages of journeymen carpenters increased, and artisanal production was an outdated, albeit highly refined, production method. On top of this came industrialisation which, with its machines and large-scale production, created a mass market. Workshop after workshop closed until only the most top-end carpentry workshops remained by the end of the 1960s.

This could have happened some years earlier, had the industry been so minded. In 1942, FDB hired the young furniture architect Børge Mogensen as head of the design studio that would distribute pieces of factory-made furniture in their thousands via consumer co-operatives across Denmark. The first major collection was launched with fanfare in 1944, and then things really took off. That same year, a consortium of furniture manufacturers, including Fritz Hansen's furniture factory, tasked the young furniture architects Hvidt & Mølgaard with designing a very similar collection of cheap furniture for export, which was named Portex (by swapping around the syllables in the word "export"). This furniture was to be sold mainly on the international market and therefore had to be either stackable or delivered in pieces. The idea in both cases was to offer complete, inviting collections of furniture that were affordable to a low-income family. This required architects to approach the task from a completely different angle. Together with the manufacturer, they had to think in terms of context and large-scale production from the very start.

In 1948, the Museum of Modern Art (MoMA) in New York announced a competition for low-cost furniture. Although several Danish furniture designers participated, none got more than an honourable mention. The winners were Robin Day from the UK and Charles Eames from the USA with furniture made of plywood and plastic. They could be mass-produced and did not require post-polishing or similar finishing. When Charles Eames's RAR chair came out of the mould, only the edge needed to be sanded.

Although there were many signs that times were changing, the master carpenters didn't see them, or didn't want to see them. Moreover, many furniture designers didn't want to acknowledge that the time for fine, unique furniture was coming to an end. Mass production largely wiped out the classic craft of cabinetmaking. It was out with woodworking benches and highly specialised carpenters, and in with uniformity and volume, alongside sexy shapes in a new aesthetic.

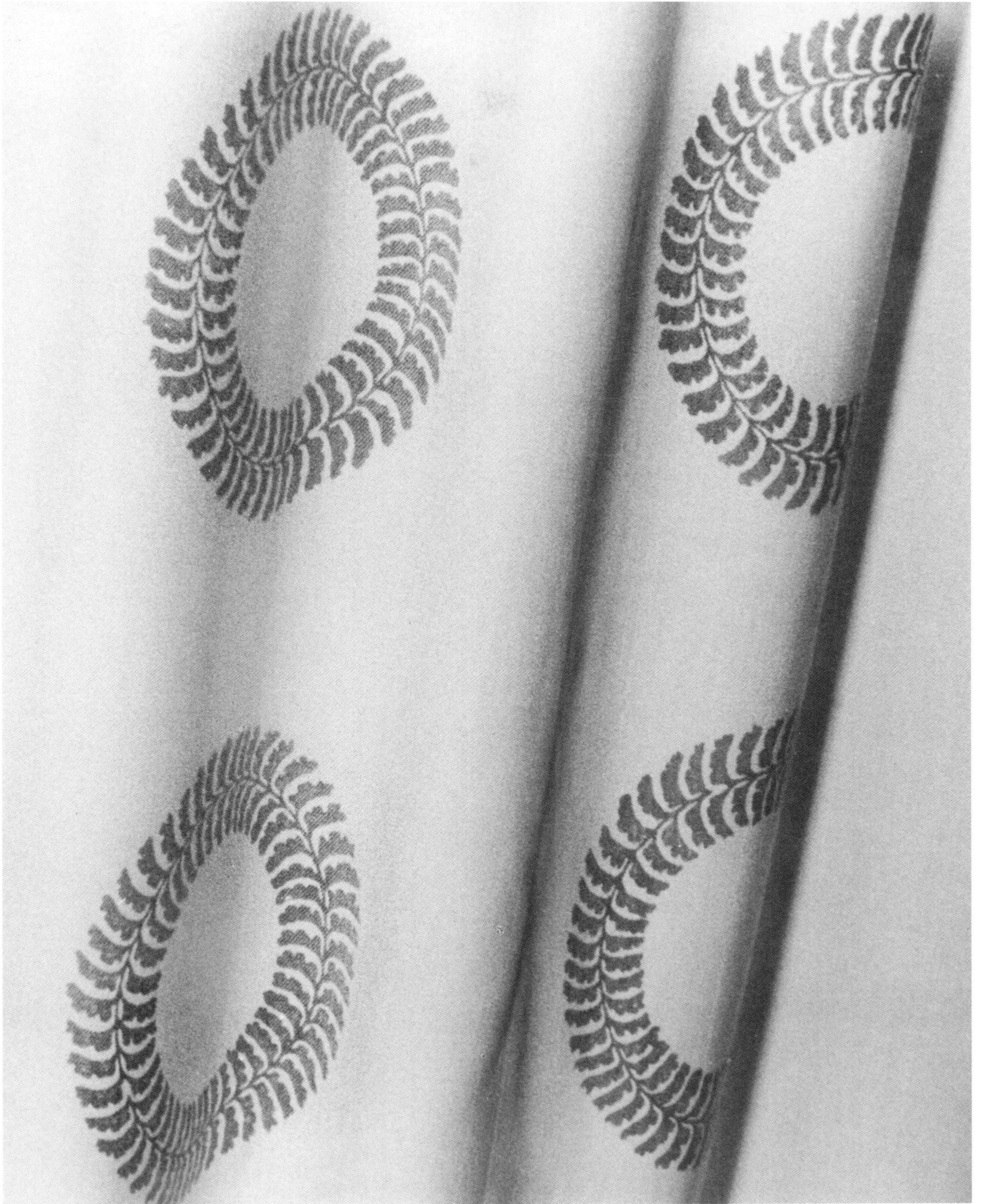

Arne makes his breakthrough

It was here, after the exhibition in 1949, that Arne Jacobsen and Fritz Hansen made their mark, and at the beginning of the 1950s a new chapter in Danish design began. For the horde of master carpenters, there was only one option for survival, and that was to become machinists in their converted carpentry workshops, or rather their newly established furniture factories.

It was a completely different mindset that emerged after the war, in the norm-forming years around 1950. Architects and manufacturers no longer thought in terms of limited orders, but in terms of endless consumption. Investments were made in machinery, and attention was paid to what was classed as modern right here and now.

Since they were producing for a broad market rather than a specific buyer, the furniture designers and manufacturers naturally had no idea whether the furniture would be a success or not. Consequently, the way that architects were remunerated also completely changed. They received royalties similar to those in the book and music industry. Furniture therefore became a bit of a gamble, as they never knew whether it would sit on the drawing board or become a hit.

With the transition from carpentry to furniture manufacturing, furniture design became the livelihood of many architects throughout the 1950s, because it became relatively easy to produce sofas, tables, and chairs on a large scale. Names like Rødkjær and Andersen from Aarhus, Ellegaards Møbelfabrik from Sejs near Silkeborg, and Slagelse Møbelværk entered their golden age. Now, however, they're forgotten, along with most of the countless furniture factories that were spawned out of carpentry workshops to feed a local furniture industry and a belief in booming exports.

The 1960s saw the closure of fine carpentry workshops and low-profile furniture factories in their droves, not only because development costs increased, but also largely because there was a shift to more modern and industrial materials such as steel and plastic. There were only a few Danish designers who could or wanted to ride the wave, and so the initiative was left to foreign manufacturers, not least the Italians. Furthermore, architects also saw a revenue stream dry up with the end of custom-made furniture.

Many architects who had made a living in furniture design right after the war instead focused on architecture and eventually became architectural design studios. This includes Hvidt and Mølgaard, who after their success with Portex continued to design many pieces of furniture for Fritz Hansen, France and Son, and Søborg Møbler. But as they headed into the 1960s, they almost completely abandoned furniture and focused instead on office buildings and the design of the new Little Belt Bridge. Other furniture designers, such as Verner Panton and Jørgen Fabricius who both had large design studios, went on to move abroad where the furniture factories were larger. They came to make a living primarily from the German furniture industry. Finally, there was what was left of the Danish scene. Here, Hans Wegner and Børge Mogensen in particular survived with their range of solid wooden chairs. But success faded towards the end for big names like Finn Juhl, who had become too expensive, too exclusive, and too old-fashioned. And Poul Kjærholm had actually not come up with any notable new furniture since his successful series for Kold Christensen in the 1950s. Jacobsen was the only one who managed to keep all his balls in the air throughout his lifetime, with both building projects and sizeable revenues from furniture.

The crème de la crème of Danish furniture design meets at the design store Den Permanente. It's 1958, and the celebrity-hungry Billed-Bladet gossip magazine has cleared an entire spread to celebrate the fact that Danish furniture sales are exceeding all expectations.

Arne Jacobsen's new design universe

On the way to Fritz Hansen's furniture factory, Søren Hansen stops his car at Jacobsen's brand new townhouse on Strandvejen. The yellow brick walls stand out against the blue sky of the late summer. There is still a smell of mortar and freshly dug soil in the garden, mixed with a little sea breeze from the Øresund, which is just on the other side of Strandvejen. The furniture manufacturer has come from his office and showroom in Christianshavn on his way to Fritz Hansen's factory in Allerød, where the beech trees are felled and dried to be turned into furniture.

Søren Hansen has a business degree, and his brother Poul Hansen is the more practical production man of the two. They own the factory together with their father, Christian Hansen. Søren Hansen has made furniture with Arne Jacobsen for many years. The curved seats in the auditorium of the Bellevue Theatre were produced by Fritz Hansen. They also designed the quirky bar stools for the large restaurant adjacent to the theatre, and together Arne Jacobsen and Fritz Hansen tried to produce an affordable restaurant chair. All before the war came.

Even though Jacobsen has a car, rationing is still in full swing in the late summer of 1952. What good is it to design a gas station for a few hundred metres further down Strandvejen when you can't fill up there due to petrol rationing? Søren Hansen can, so Jacobsen leaves his car at home. They're going to a meeting up at the factory with the operations engineers and Poul Hansen – the father will probably also be there.

Søren Hansen opens the door with the newly polished brass sign with 'Jacobsen' written in cursive script. He intentionally overlooks the more modest sign next to it: 'To the design studio' with a downward arrow, referring to the basement door by the garage. Here's where the employees are sat, the draughtsmen – including Verner Panton, who helps bring the new chair to life.

The meeting at the factory is to approve the new chair, which they've been working on for almost a year. Jacobsen stands ready in the entrance foyer. They exchange a few polite phrases – there's more to talk about in the car. The dry spell when it comes to construction projects persists. Granted, there's the youth housing project and a school on Fyn, as well as all the competitions. Although it's seven years since the war, it can still be felt, Jacobsen laments. The villa construction projects, which were such a big part of his design studio before the war, have almost ceased. Even his own townhouse was built using government loans. The textiles are doing nicely and selling well, especially abroad. Arne also comments on how he and Jonna are still making more patterns. And thankfully there's still the interior of Novo's canteen. Jacobsen makes it clear that it is solely a surplus of time that has enabled him to make this new little chair.

They now turn into the factory's courtyard in Allerød. Like most of them, it's a somewhat anonymous factory complex that has sprouted up with the large visible pipework typical of the timber industry. The sounds of whining circular saws add to the atmosphere. Inside the meeting room stands the prototype for the small three-legged chair that has been so difficult to make.

Engineers Svend Villumsen and Hans Engholm have been working on it for a year. They're responsible for the innovative technique that Fritz Hansen has developed for steam bending and plywood. Two years earlier, together with the young furniture architects Orla Mølgaard-Nielsen and Peter Hvidt, they had developed the AX chair, where the seat shell was bent in two directions. However, their chair was divided into a seat and a back. That chair had attracted justifiable international attention and had become a commercial success, but to Hvidt and Mølgaard's disdain, the famous Arne Jacobsen has now come to the fore at Fritz Hansen with his new concept.

A chair formed from a single piece of plywood mounted on a frame of tubular steel – this was roughly how Jacobsen had explained his idea to Søren Hansen over the phone. A small, lightweight chair that could be used in modern home decor. It could fit into the myriad of apartment blocks of two and three-room apartments that he himself had helped build before the war, and which everyone now expected would be the housing style of the future. A chair for the apartment's dining room or the more modern kitchen-diner, where the kitchen and dining room flow into one. Not to mention that any extra chairs could form a decorative stack in a corner.

First there was the shape itself. What would it look like? The starting point was a simple design that began life as anything but an hourglass shape at the start of the process. It looked too much like the chair designed by the Ray and Charles Eames, which was produced by the US competitor Herman Miller. Their chair had been painstakingly imported from the US as part of a competitor analysis. The shape of Jacobsen's chair was therefore changed to be much more dynamic with an almost circular seat and an oval back connected by a straight transition piece between them. Time and again, the engineers had folded, bent, and broken the chair at the lumbar point. That was until Jacobsen came up with the idea of the curved notch, which gave the organic waist shape.

One issue was that Jacobsen wasn't especially easy to work with. He did not come with a finished chair, rather with a feeling for the shape of a chair, and certainly not a solution for its construction. The prototype had been back and forth between the factory and the design studio many times. The model had been amended over and over again with pencil strokes, so much so that Verner Panton was getting tired of all the changes. In the end, the amendments became so minor that the foreman up at Fritz Hansen simply erased the line on the model and sent it back for approval.

The frame also posed its own challenges. Eames' chairs had 16 mm tubes, but Jacobsen had to reduce his to 14 mm. Could you even see a difference? Jacobsen persisted. 14 mm it was, and the difference was clear. The ingenious thing about the frame was the way it was attached to the shell, with three screws into a small circular plywood plate that was mounted just below the centre of the seat. In addition, the rubber discs were placed a little further out and finally there was a simple cover in light grey plastic with the company name moulded in. Simple, robust, and resilient. It was a very elegant way to assemble the components. It was arguably here that the efforts of the technically skilled Verner Panton really came into play.

Another crucial problem was how much the plywood could be twisted in three dimensions without the seat shell splitting or breaking. During the first years, the mould had to be replaced nine or ten times in order to change, adjust, and refine the chair. The elegance of the seat shell became more and more pronounced. First, they tried pressing tools made of wood, without any kind of hardening aids. It took up to three days to get the shell stiff enough before the mould could be disassembled. Not very industrial, nor cheap. The curing time was significantly reduced once the factory invested in expensive aluminium moulds with flowing hot water. It was a development project that had been so difficult that Fritz Hansen's only designer – the newly hired architect Poul Kjærholm – left suddenly, deeply frustrated. He had worked for the company for a year on a number of projects, including a curved recliner. But there was never the time or money for Kjærholm's furniture to enter the development phase and be realised.

The chassis assembly on the seat shell of an early version of the three-legged *Ant*. Later, an improved assembly was developed, which was also hidden by a bowl-shaped plastic shell that simply had to be clicked into place.

Here it was – a slender frame with three thin legs, together with the various tables that were developed at the same time, including a small egg-shaped model intended for a mum, dad, and children in a small apartment. The new chair had been given the rather bland name: 3100. Though beautiful and well-shaped, it was far too expensive. Jacobsen was satisfied with his chair and jovially announced that he had sold almost 200 for Novo's new canteen at just under DKK 50 each. Søren Hansen claimed that Fritz Hansen had intended to sell it for DKK 55, as it had been *very* expensive to develop. Jacobsen snorted and stood firm at 50. Would anyone want it if it was more than 50?

Søren and Christian Hansen dug their heels in and said that Arne would have to pay part of the development costs himself or accept lower royalties if he was insistent on a price of DKK 50. Jacobsen grabbed the chair and headed for the door. "I'll find another manufacturer!" he shouted. Søren Hansen blocked the door: "That chair stays here! It's as much ours as it is yours," he shouted and continued: "It may be your design, but it's our technology! We won't let that go." Like a spoilt child who was always used to getting his way, Jacobsen left the meeting, speechless with anger.

Jacobsen came home late that day. He didn't have a car, so he took the train from Allerød to Klampenborg. The long journey gave him time to think. He had made so many chairs, as well as lamps and clocks. But never like this. The design of the chair had led him to a place where he was helplessly dependent on others, on large investments, and on industrial machinery.

But it also brought the promising mass market within reach, just as it did for the textiles that he and Jonna had made for the Swedes a few years earlier. Fritz Hansen had sold 800 of Hvidt & Mølgaard's AX chairs per month to the US alone! What couldn't be achieved?

Jacobsen received a 5% royalty of the retail price of DKK 50, i.e. DKK 2.50. Due to the high development costs, it has not since been index-linked. So the royalties on this chair remained at the 1952 level – DKK 2.50. It was with this chair that Jacobsen's life as an iconic designer commenced. When the 3100 was presented in the autumn of 1952 in connection with Fritz Hansen A/S's 80th anniversary, it was well received and given the nickname the *Ant*.

← Jacobsen originally argued that the *Ant* should be launched as a lightweight stackable chair for new post-war homes with more limited space.

Here you can see three examples around the small oval table that was launched at the same time as the *Ant*. There's space for mum, dad, and a couple of kids in the new, small apartment.

The *Ant* in the veneered version with three legs. The name comes mostly from the shape of the seat shell with its round curves and characteristic waist, but also the three thin legs, which were seen as very flimsy at the time the chair was launched. So flimsy that some

people refused to sit on the chair, convinced it would collapse beneath them. The chair was also criticised for tipping over easily with its three legs, to which Jacobsen defended himself by saying that it had five legs, because you have two of your own.

Shell chairs are the new style

In the early 1950s, Europe is still living in the shadow of the Second World War, but society is slowly returning to normal. Or rather a 'new normal', as the war turned everything upside down, waged immense destruction, while also heralding the breakthrough of new ideas, technologies, and materials. Design and architecture are undergoing major upheavals. The old modernism produced by the likes of Bauhaus, Le Corbusier, and Kaare Klint in the interwar years, now seemed a bit passé. A softer and more humane functionalism, inspired by natural shapes and aerodynamic airplanes, began to emerge out of the earlier, somewhat rigid and machine-like functionalism.

↑ Fritz Hansen's approach to furniture was clearly different from that of many other furniture manufacturers of the time. The furniture was light and largely industrially manufactured. Plywood and steam-bent wood were used extensively. Just a few examples are shown here: The Canada chair designed by Christian Hansen himself could be embellished with loose cushions. There's also Søren Hansen's *Series 7*-like chair, which formed the basis for Jacobsen's *Series 7* shell chair a few years later.

↓ The AX chair was designed just after the war by architects Hvidt & Mølgaard as a self-assembly chair for export. Moulded plywood was used to make the seat and back of the chair. It is this lamination technique that was further developed to make the *Ant* a few years later.

Although the new furniture was far from accepted by the general public right away, the trend was unavoidable. It was in this time of change that Jacobsen chose to enter the scene with his small, light chair at a reasonable price. At the start of the 1950s, both Henning Larsen and Verner Panton were employed at the design studio for a time – exactly when the *Ant* was developed. Panton in particular became heavily involved in the process. He initially made a series of small models in bent steel wire, which were displayed on a box next to his drawing table. One of these was sent to a blacksmith to be made into a full-size model, but when it proved to be very heavy and unwieldy, it was discarded in the doorway to the design studio – it was just too clumsy.

Through Fritz Hansen, they then acquired one of the Eames's first chairs, where the seat and back were produced in laminated wood in two separate parts and mounted onto chrome-plated steel frame. Fritz Hansen was thereby involved in the project from a fairly early stage and was also the Danish furniture company with the most experience in laminating veneer for furniture parts.

A number of shell chairs were designed after the *Ant*, and gradually Fritz Hansen became more skilled at bending wood into all sorts of profiles. The equilibrist *Grand Prix* chair from 1957 was the only small shell chair to have a wooden underframe. The legs are made of laminated veneer and milled into shape afterwards. The name is due to the fact that the chair won the Grand Prix at the design triennale in Milan the same year it was launched.

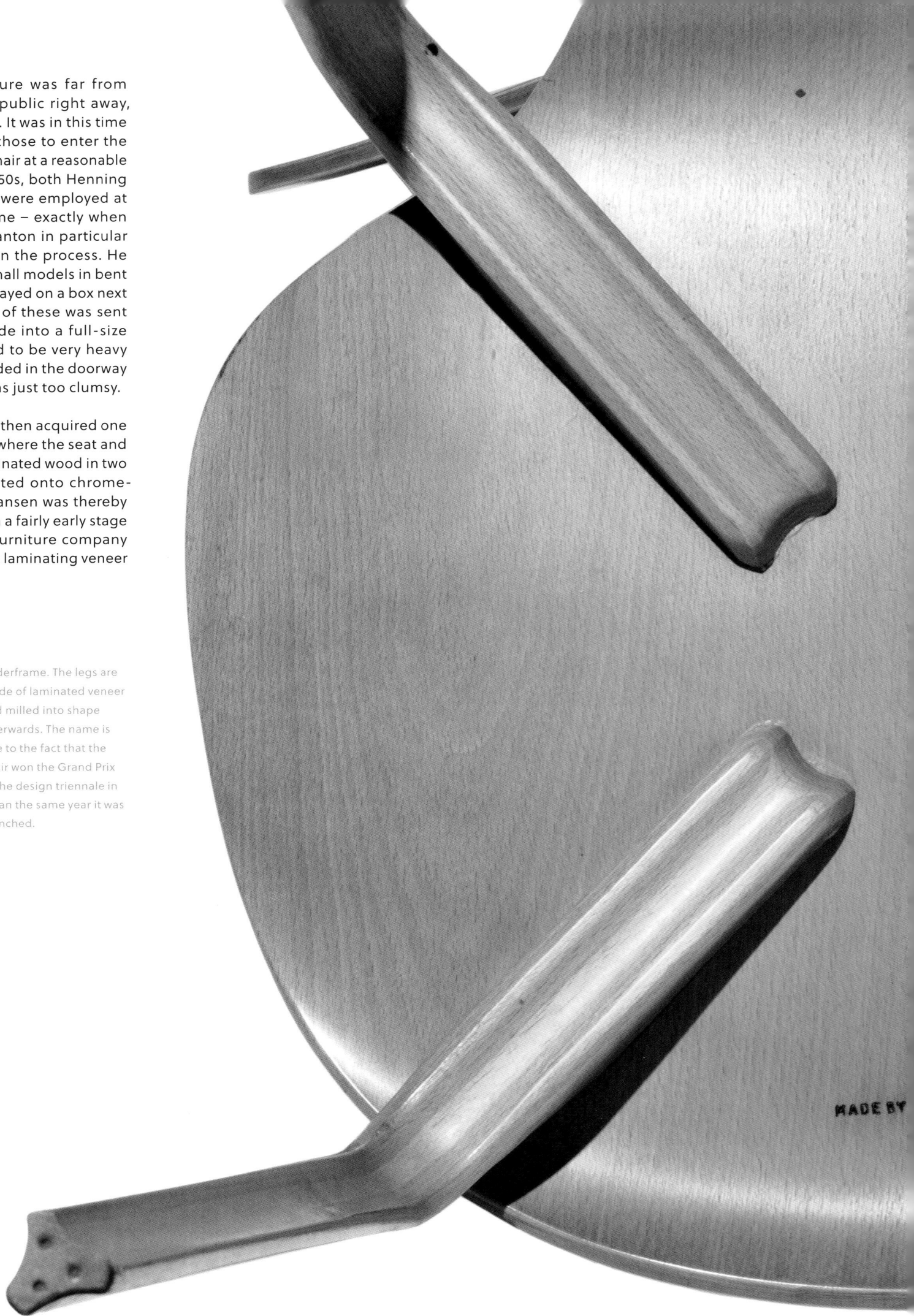

MADE BY

It wasn't completely new, after all. For example, around 1930, Alvar Aalto had started to develop his well-known birch veneer furniture made using this technology. The aircraft industry had heavily pursued lamination technology during the war by experiment with things like new types of glue. In this way wood could, in some cases, replace expensive metal in the production of aircraft fuselages. A well-known example is the ultra-fast fighter plane – the de Havilland Mosquito – that bombed the Shell building in Copenhagen. It was built from laminated wood by trained carpenters from the British furniture industry, who swapped industries during the war.

In the late 1930s, Ray and Charles Eames had worked on laminating parts for furniture. During the war they came to manufacture stretchers and shin guards out of laminated wood for the US Navy.

Jacobsen had also used laminated wooden shells for the rows of chairs in the Bellevue theatre, which he designed in 1937, but these only curved in one direction (in principle, like a section of a cylindrical shape). The same can be said of Alvar Aalto's furniture for the most part. This didn't represent any major technological challenge. In contrast, double-curved surfaces were a somewhat more challenging task, both in development and production. Veneer behaves a bit like a ream of paper, easy to bend in one direction, but much more difficult to shape in two directions at once, such as into a bowl-shaped chair seat. To bend the veneer in two directions, you may need to cut slits in the layers, which is how the Eames made their stretchers and shin guards for the US Navy. But it's not quite as durable and doesn't look as attractive as if you can get the veneer to stay intact.

This was the great challenge for Jacobsen, Verner Panton, and Fritz Hansen – how much curvature can be achieved by manipulating veneer, glue, and moulding tools without the finished wooden shell splitting? To create a continuous seat shell, back, and seat in one, Jacobsen wanted to push the limits of what the material and technology could handle. Therefore, the final *Ant* was bent in two directions as much as was technically possible at the time. The seat shell was made as thin as possible without breaking under the load of a human body, and the steel tube frame was also made to be as flimsy as possible. Consequently the *Ant* has the characteristic waist at the bottom of its back, because it's here that the veneer layers must be pressed together the most and where some material had to be removed to prevent the shell from splitting.

Jacobsen couldn't foresee this issue before he went to Fritz Hansen with some sketches and a sales pitch about the small stackable chair.

For him, the most important thing was that it was aesthetically pleasing, well-proportioned, solid, distinctive, and a popular piece of design that would be noticed. He therefore insisted that everything should be as he saw fit.

The contour of the chair should have the right beautiful curves. Whereas the *Dan* chair from 1933 and its prototype, the Viennese chair, have a flat seat, the *Ant*'s seat is such a precise saucer shape that the resulting bowl provides good seating comfort. It's much better than the Eames chair, where the seat is just flat and not particularly springy when you sit in it. This is where Jacobsen's design excels with its springy back – probably a feature that the development team didn't expect when they started the development process, but which they welcomed with open arms. Jacobsen himself highlighted the dynamic nature of the chair in a later interview with a British journalist when he mentioned that it has five legs – despite having three legs of its own, its small seat forces you to sit with your legs spread apart, and you contribute the last two legs yourself in order to maintain balance.

The interaction between figure and background is the key to understanding all graphics. There's the black text, and then there's the white in the space in between. That was the graphic trick that Jacobsen exploited in his designs.

The space between two shell chairs when placed next to each other creates a distinct shape that is just as important as the main shape itself. Here, for example, we see the well-shaped *Series 7* chairs and their calm undulating rhythm as they stand in rows at a medical congress in the Bella Center in the 1970s.

Experiences from exile in Sweden

Jacobsen had learnt something from his foray into textiles during his exile in Sweden. He understood that you could work with industrial production without necessarily sacrificing quality and aesthetics. The textiles and wallpapers were mass-produced consumables, not manual handicrafts. And if you prepared properly, took the task seriously, and found the best manufacturers and subcontractors, the industry could actually deliver something that was at least as good as what an artisan could produce – sometimes perhaps even better. However, you had to know the rules and understand that mass production requires large investments in moulds, tools, and sometimes special machines. Jacobsen had begun to realise this in Sweden. He accepted these rules, first with the textiles in Sweden and then with the *Ant* and his subsequent furniture.

Jacobsen's design concept changed during this time, and partly also his working methods. He therefore entered a completely new phase in his design career and left the carpentry tradition that he had followed before the war.

Something else Jacobsen had learnt in Sweden was to cultivate an organic design language in his designs. It was initially flowers and plants that served as the basis for the design of his textiles and wallpapers. The organic patterns later became increasingly abstract, which is how his furniture also came to look.

The *Ant* doesn't look like an ant, really. It was its 'waist', slender legs, and small size that, at an exhibition in 1953, led Finn Juhl to compare the chair to an ant – a name that stuck.

The abrupt interruption in Jacobsen's career due to his exile in Sweden helped to revive his artistic fascination with the curved and soft forms of nature, further influenced by his marriage to Jonna. His old interest in nature and painting nature motifs suddenly turned out to be increasingly useful. Initially, it translated into naturalistic motifs in textile prints, and then into a more organically inspired design language in his three-dimensional designs.

Where would Arne Jacobsen have been without Søren Hansen's counterpoint? Probably not the prominent furniture designer he became. Many different pieces of furniture passed through Fritz Hansen's production system. From the Hansen brothers' own chair designs such as the affordable Canada armchair to the cheap Danish-folk style Dan chair, which came in many variants somewhat in the vein of the Vienna chair. Fritz Hansen also made upholstered furniture that didn't particularly stand out. From the early 1930s, they began developing more refined furniture from Danish furniture architects, including the *Church Chair* by Kaare Klint, for use in Grundtvig Church, but the architect Frits Schlegel also created large collections at a more affordable price.

Søren Hansen was also a talent scout who brought young furniture designers into the fold and gave them a chance. Poul Kjærholm, Nanna Ditzel, and Verner Panton all started their careers at Fritz Hansen with their first pieces of furniture. But at the same time, Fritz Hansen, still with Søren Hansen at the helm, developed a policy that included development and sales right from the start of the design process. And development wasn't just a foreman, an experienced carpenter, and a planer. It involved highly qualified engineers who thought in terms of design, who were innovative, and who could push the production equipment to its limits, while ensuring that the design was profitable.

Søren Hansen participated in international symposia, where he was inspired by the Anglo-Saxon concept of industrial design, where design is combined with the capabilities of the production system, sales needs, and feedback. He was also involved in the Carpenters' Guild exhibitions together with alderman A.J. Iversen as his counterpart. There was a big discussion in the 1950s – in the midst of Danish Modern's success, the winning partnership was now to be found between the carpenter with their craftsmanship and the artistically minded architect. Or, as Søren Hansen put it, the path shifted from furniture design to industrial design. So the very concept of industrial design, which Jacobsen did not like, was pivotal for Fritz Hansen's success.

Applied arts is a very special form of production that has formed the basis for all the large Danish companies that care about design. Of course, here we're talking about Fritz Hansen, but others include Bang & Olufsen, LEGO, and Georg Jensen. They are all driven by a symbiosis of business, innovation and, not least, sublime aesthetic understanding, with bold and innovative designs.

Although few companies in the Danish furniture industry of the 1950s followed this line of thinking, France og Søn in Hillerød was perhaps one of them. France og Søn was spawned from the Lama mattress factory with Brit Fearnley France at the helm. His starting point was the production of mini mattresses that could be used as backs and pillows for his knock-down furniture. He strongly believed in the rational assembly line technique, but still made use of exquisite materials and the best architects such as Finn Juhl and Hvidt and Mølgaard as in-house designers. But France og Søn didn't survive the owner-manager retiring some 15 to 20 years later.

Another wooden goods factory that survived by thinking innovatively and following the flow of the market was LEGO, which ultimately ended up in toy production with the slogan LEG GODT – LE-GO.

At first it was an ordinary carpentry shop that made windows and ladders. When the crisis of the 1930s came, this turned into smaller versions of ladders and ironing boards for children, which then finally morphed into purely wooden toys. After the war, the new material plastic and the LEGO brick came along, and the rest is history.

Kay Bojesen followed in the same footsteps with a large range of wooden toys, but he did not think commercially in the same way and remained in the sphere of applied arts with fine exhibitions and great applause from critics who wrote about his craftsmanship. There's the extraordinary, and then there's the execution.

None of these companies achieved this overnight; they adapted themselves and their ideas to become stronger and stronger. And they used talented designers, of course. But designers are not God-given creators. They work by way of a sounding board made up of a team of specialists. And when the right team is in place, they can create masterpieces: in collaboration with others, never alone.

The Hansen family at the 75th anniversary of the factory in 1947. Christian E. Hansen on the right and in bronze portrait. Sons Søren on the far-left and Fritz next to him. This is just before the Danish Modern's big breakthrough.

The *Ant* was a major breakthrough for both Jacobsen and for lamination technology. The chair has been an icon in the global furniture and design community ever since. Having the *Ant* standing in your home or in your company's canteen was seen as the epitome of modernity and culture – you were definitely at the forefront of the trends of the time. It didn't stop with this minimalist three-legged chair. Both Jacobsen and Fritz Hansen wanted more – they wanted to leverage their success and the newly developed technology to provide more opportunities and more revenues.

In other words, there was a need for a more usable and perhaps also more marketable chair. The *Ant*, as groundbreaking as it was, had some issues – it was quite small and flimsy, and only had three legs. Jacobsen insisted for a long time that the *Ant* should not come in a four-legged version – it should be as small and simple as possible. The problem with having only one front leg was that it risked falling over. This was a particular risk if it was freestanding and the person leant forwards. They could fall flat on their face if the chair toppled over. If used in a canteen, such as at Novo, where you typically sit at a table and eat, nothing usually happened because you had the table to lean your elbows on.

Another problem with the *Ant* was that it could not be upholstered due to the complex profile of the backrest. Fritz Hansen had tried to develop a fixed thin felt cushion for the seat, but it didn't work very well. In other words, a new variant of the shell chair was needed, and Jacobsen and his employees set to work on it in 1955. This chair was given the product name 3107, which later became the *Series 7*, partly because of the silhouette of the backrest, with the right-hand side resembling a number 7. Since then, Fritz Hansen has called the chair and its various variants the *Series 7*.

← In response to customers' needs and wishes, a multitude of variants of the shell chairs were developed, including a hymnbook holder on the back or a writing table to the front. It was primarily the *Series 7* that gained different variants, but other Jacobsen models were also modified. Here you can see the ergonomic *T-chair*, which is mounted on a column and equipped with a writing table. It might have been for a conference centre or university.

Most of Jacobsen's chairs are known by their nickname, except for the *Series 7* chair. It was Fritz Hansen's product name 3107 that inspired the name *Series 7* and possibly also the characteristic profile of the backrest which, with a little imagination, could well resemble the number 7. The chair was the practical and comfortable version of the *Ant*, because it could accommodate the butt and back. The chair was quietly introduced at a major architecture and housing exhibition in Helsingborg in 1955 in two versions – with and without armrests. The version with armrests was Jacobsen's own favourite.

But in reality, the *Series 7* may have had a precursor at Fritz Hansen as early as the 1930s. Based in part on Thonet's café chairs, which Fritz Hansen had purchased the licensing rights to manufacture, Søren Hansen had developed the Dan chair, which became Fritz Hansen's own take on a Viennese chair, and which went into production in 1933. The idea was to create a popular, affordable, and practical chair that could be used in halls, community centres, and canteens. The chair was designed in such a way that the back could be customised, while the seat and base were always the same. This means that the chair could change its appearance depending on the task – and that was something the architects could use. Magnus Stephensen and Vilhelm Lauritzen each made their own version. The canteen of Radiohuset was furnished with Vilhelm Lauritzen's version.

But Jacobsen didn't use this model for his version of the *Series 7*, or did he? Søren Hansen himself made several versions of the Dan chair, including one from 1942, which had the *Series 7*'s back. Jacobsen probably had knowledge of all these variant types. Whether he was directly involved in this version and perhaps rejected it for use in his town and city halls is not known. It may have been included in Fritz Hansen's product range as their own design. What is certain is that once the *Ant* had been fully developed in 1952 and the larger *Series 7* model was being explored, it was the factory's Dan chair that was used as the basis for its back design ... an almost direct copy.

The *Series 7* had four legs from the beginning – a three-legged version was not on the cards here. It had to be stable and attract a wider audience, so it was given four legs and a slightly wider seat shell, which can be seen on both the seat and the backrest. The increased size and stability made it easier for the user to sit and relax, as well as change positions without the fear of falling over. The chair has the same construction as its predecessor, the *Ant*, in all other key respects. The laminated seat shell is made in the same way and with the same thickness. Moreover, it's stackable. The legs are the same type and fitted with the same hard rubbery blocks under the seat, both to ensure stability and to prevent scratches on the seat underneath when stacking.

The *Series 7* came in two versions – with and without armrests. Jacobsen's favourite was the chair with arms, which was highlighted at the launch at the major H55 design and architecture exhibition in Helsingborg in 1955.

Jacobsen had considerable influence on the set-up of this exhibition. In the main exhibition, only the version with armrests was displayed, while the version without could only be seen in the Danish apartment, which Finn Juhl was responsible for furnishing. These two editions were just the beginning of the development of the system that became the *Series 7*. Over the years that followed, new variants were designed, including an office chair with a completely different base and equipped with wheels.

Later, a waiting room version was also released, where the base with legs was replaced with a single, sturdy column that could be bolted to the floor. A coupling bracket to be mounted under the seat was also manufactured so that the *Series 7* could be set up in long, stable rows for auditorium use. For school and conference use, a writing table was produced to replace the right armrest. A tall version, like a bar stool, was also designed. Curiously, a miniature version is also available as a children's chair. The *Series 7* was initially produced with either veneered surfaces (rosewood, oak, or teak) or in a black lacquered version and in various upholstered versions. Later, several new colour options were created both by Jacobsen himself in 1968, and subsequently by Verner Panton in 1972 and Poul Gernes in 1988.

The *Series 7* thereby became Jacobsen's first experience with actual system design. Where the *Ant* was a victory in the battle with materials and technology, and designed in an artistically distinctive way, the *Series 7* became the more popular chair characterised by pragmatism and systematicity. It is more capable, which is reflected in the significantly higher production figures compared to that of the *Ant*. Furthermore, the different versions enabled Fritz Hansen to gain a larger market share, both in the private market and in particular in the contract market.

Throughout the 1960s, the factory regularly attempted to refine the capabilities of the *Series 7*. They experimented with fiberglass to replace the laminated wood shell. But it was never as strong as the Eames's chair or the Panton chair for that matter, which has a lip-shaped bend all the way around the shell. On the other hand, the *Series 7*'s seat shell had to be as thin as possible, also at the edge, meaning it would not be strong enough to support a person's weight. They also tried an airport bench, where shells were placed on a central beam, and other variants.

A variant of Jacobsen's shell chair was nicknamed the *Tongue* due to the shape of the seat shell. It was introduced in 1955, the same year as several other lightweight laminated chairs, including the *Series 7*. The *Tongue* differs radically from all the other models in that it cannot be stacked due to the Sputnik-like design of the chassis. It was intended as a school chair and was used at Munkegård school when it was inaugurated in 1957. Initially, the backrest had an asymmetrically placed hole milled into the back, so it was easier to handle, especially for children. However, the fact that the *Tongue* could not be stacked made it less practical, and it was discontinued after a few years.

The school chair that ended up being used as the standard chair at Munkegård school was called the *Mosquito*. It came in three sizes, with accompanying desks, and it had a very narrow back, which extended out into some dorsal fins. These also functioned as a kind of handle that made the chair easy to handle.

Jacobsen worked on several other shell chair models almost simultaneously while developing the *Series 7*. Two chairs were designed for Munkegård school in Gentofte, which the design studio began working on in 1949 and which were finally completed in 1957. One of the chairs differs radically from the other Jacobsen shell chairs in that it could not be stacked. It was nicknamed the *Tongue* because of its distinctive seat shell design, but had the official name 3106 at Fritz Hansen (later it was called 3102).

The legs of the tongue are straight and protrude diagonally from a centre point under the seat in a sputnik-like design that was very popular at the time. Sputnik was the first man-made satellite to orbit Earth, and its spherical shape had spiky antennae radiating from a central point. The seat shell was laminated in the same way as the other shell chairs, but completely lacked the waist-like narrowing at the bottom of the back that the other chairs in the family had. On the other hand, the *Tongue* had a lumbar curve, which provided a more ergonomic seating position for some people. It was designed in 1955 as Munkegård school neared completion. It was the smallest Jacobsen chair – also compared to the other shell chairs in the series. It was initially only produced for the Munkegård project and had a bean-shaped hole at the top of the back piece that served as a handle, and which was also slightly asymmetrically offset to the right.

← A loudspeaker was also designed for Munkegård school. Every classroom was equipped with one. The design was very modern for its time and consisted simply of a heat-pressed plexiglass plate that held four speaker units. It was awarded the Grand Prix at the Triennale

in Milan and, a few years later, was the starting point for Jacobsen to begin a small collaboration with Braun, for which he designed a speaker. Also visible is the built-in ceiling lamp, which was named the *Munkegaard Lamp*.

↑ The school desk for Munkegård school uses the same materials as the shell chairs: Laminated veneer and a tubular steel frame. The advantage of the veneer shell is that it can be easily designed to create a small shelf under the tabletop.

↓ The Munkegård school project enabled Jacobsen to cultivate one of his passions: gardens. The school's classrooms were positioned like contour lines, which created a small courtyard for each class, which the children could go use during their breaks.

The second chair designed for Munkegård school was model 3105. It was nicknamed the *Mosquito* and is also known as the *Munkegaard Chair*. It solved a problem with the *Ant* and *Series 7*, namely that they were a bit difficult to get a grip on due to the somewhat awkward design of the backrest.

The *Mosquito* had two wings or handles at the top of the back piece, which made it easier to grab the chair to move it, especially for the children. Otherwise, the chair does not differ much from the two previously mentioned versions. The shell is laminated in the same way, and the chassis is the same as the *Series 7* so it can be easily stacked. In addition to the normal adult size, the *Mosquito* came in two smaller versions to accommodate the different age groups among school students. It had a veneered surface as standard and gained a degree of popularity, especially in schools and other public spaces. The adult version was a bit flimsy and not particularly sturdy, while the smaller children's variants were somewhat more durable. Production continued until the end of the 1960s and expanded to include an office chair with the same base as the *Series 7*'s office edition.

← The adult-sized *Mosquito*. It's rather unclear how and why it got its nickname, but it was a successor to the *Ant* and perhaps has a shape that could be somewhat reminiscent of the mosquito's body, with its wings and legs.

→ The curtain for the stage in the hall at Munkegård school. Large and jolly, with a colourful harlequin pattern. Unfortunately, the school hall was later rebuilt with a large, dominating staircase, so the space now feels like a confused area of activity. The original school hall was one of Jacobsen's most successful rooms. Opposite the stage, there was originally a glass wall that had a lightweight curtain with the same pattern in front. In addition, there were a multitude of chairs and a lectern, where a slanted skylight illuminated a smiling principal as they welcomed the new students.

← Six *Grand Prix* chairs around a dining table. This is probably the design where Jacobsen draws most from the world-renowned Danish Modern. A finely crafted arrangement in teak that leaves the other Danish manufacturers in the dust.

Over the years, many have complained about the seating comfort of Jacobsen's various shell chairs. Shortly after the *Ant*'s launch in 1952, chief physician Dr. Egill Snorrason pointed out that the shell chairs lacked adequate lumbar support. Jacobsen listened to the criticism and, with Snorrason as a consultant, model 3103 was designed in 1955. It has been called the *T-chair* because of the characteristic contour of the backrest. Seen from the side we can see that it differs significantly ergonomically from the other chairs. A slight bend in the profile reveals its unique and ergonomic lumbar support. Several versions of the *T-chair* were in production until the end of the 1960s – two with a lower seat height for school use, a version with a writing table, an office chair with a swivel base and wheels, and a version with a central column for fixing to the floor, such as in a vestibule.

↑ In response to criticism from a chief physician specialising in ergonomics, Jacobsen designed a new shell chair in 1955, the *T-chair*, which has a different curve in the back. It has better lumbar support, which appears as a small inward 'buckle' on the back. The *T-chair* could also be lifted and moved more easily due to the T-shaped seat shell. It was only in production for a few years.

↓ A classroom at Munkegård school with the original desks and a view of the courtyard. The row of high windows on the left is an innovation in school architecture for this time. The advantage is that more light enters the otherwise rather dark right side of the room.

The *Grand Prix* chair with its characteristic legs in laminated wood. There was also a version with a chassis like the *Series 7*, made of thin steel tubes. The back of the *Grand Prix* chair resembled three spokes emanating from a central point.

This motif is repeated in the cross-section of the characteristic legs in laminated wood. Together with the loudspeaker from Munkegård school, it also won the Grand Prix at the Triennale in Milan.

Parallel to the development of the *Ant* in 1951-52, Jacobsen designed another furniture series built from tubular steel frames and laminated wooden elements, probably also in this case with assistance from the young Verner Panton. A whole small family of furniture was manufactured by the carpentry firm Rud. Rasmussen in Nørrebro in Copenhagen. Although the buyer was a foundation in New York – the Scandinavian-American Society – it was the large Copenhagen shipyard Burmeister og Wain that paid for Jacobsen's design and Rud. Rasmussen's production of a small run of the furniture (ten pieces of each, according to the factory's archives) by way of a donation to the foundation. The furniture was shipped to the US in 1952.

The series, also called *Scan-Am* furniture, consisted of a desk with a drawer module and a fixed, rotatable table lamp, as well as an almost identical tea table that was slightly shorter and had no drawers. In addition, a three-legged armchair was developed into a two-seater sofa. Although an office chair was not designed for this series, in old photos an *Ant* chair has been used to complement the desk. The common feature of this furniture series was the bent, matt chrome-plated steel tube frames and the black wooden parts which, in the case of the chairs, were upholstered on the front. Although they perhaps did not reach the level of the other shell chairs in terms of their functionality and aesthetic simplicity, they were nevertheless striking pieces of furniture.

The desk top was made of solid wood with a top layer of smoked rosewood veneer. It is so refined that it looks as if the top is made of laminated wood that has been bent down around the frame. The top of the legs is seen in a kind of slit in the corners, and it is this effect in particular that gives the table its distinctive soft character. Another important detail is the hinged side table for the typewriter. This can be swung away when not in use and when the user needs to reach into the drawers. The typewriter can then be pulled out again as needed. The drawer module is suspended as a free-floating element on either the left or right side. This was an effect that Finn Juhl had used in his own design studio furniture from 1945, and which gives the furniture an elegant visual lightness. Finally, on the left side of the tabletop, there is a small storage module with the aforementioned integrated swivelling table lamp.

↓ A sample set-up of the *Scan-Am* furniture before shipment to New York. Here we can see most of the *Scan-Am* series combined with the *Ant* and the curtain *Trapez*. Rud. Rasmussens Snedkerier took care of the complicated desk with a swivel table for a typewriter and a built-in lamp, along with the lounge chair and sofa.

→ After countless sketches, Jacobsen designed this lounge chair for Rud. Rasmussens Snedkerier. The chair was part of a small series called *Scan-Am*. However, it was quite unstable when you tried to get up from it, so it remained a niche product.

In 1950, Arne and Jonna moved from their temporary townhouse home at Sløjfen 21 in Jægersborg. They had lived here for five years after returning from Sweden while their new home at Bellevue was built. The new townhouse, Strandvejen 413, was built by Jacobsen together with a consortium of contractors. To minimise costs, he designed a row of four terraced houses. He and Jonna lived in the end one with a view over Bellevue beach from the first floor. Many architects at the time used the same principle – design a handful of houses and get your own home instead of earning a fee.

It is in the same area where Jacobsen designed his earlier white apartment buildings, theatre, and the bathing lake. Jacobsen had previously outlined how the entire area, from Skovshoved to the zoo at Tårbæk, could be built and landscaped. Proposals for high-rise buildings at Skovshoved harbour and the observation tower at Dyrehaven were not realised, to the joy of many.

It was a small house that the Jacobsens had plans to move into. When it was designed in 1946, it was to be 110 square metres in order to be eligible for a government loan, but by the time it was completed in 1950, it had expanded to 160 square metres. There was also a complete basement – but not for groceries or storage rooms. In fact there were 6 to 8 draughtsmen sat down here. They were young and ambitious architects working in the fully equipped design studio with poor lighting and certainly no beach views. They weren't to be distracted while working. In one corner, Jacobsen sat enthroned in his glass enclosure like any other foreman, with a specially designed inbox where the draughtsmen could quietly submit the day's work for approval. A table was reserved for furniture development, and it was here that Verner Panton sat and completed his work on the first chairs and accompanying tables for Fritz Hansen.

As in any other commercial enterprise in the province, every room in the house, from the basement to the attic, was buzzing with life and hard work. On the ground floor, one of the reception rooms was quickly converted into the admin office to manage the frequent correspondence with clients and enquiries about photographic materials for exhibitions and magazines, which was an important part of the marketing of Arne Jacobsen as an architectural firm. Since only Jonna's teenage daughter Gitte was still living at home, the second reception room was also used as a drawing room, where the furniture and other designs could be developed in peace. A living room had been turned into a meeting room and upstairs, next to the living room, Jonna sat working on the extensive collections of textiles with a view and a fireplace.

Several young architects were hired along the way, and when the house itself soon became too small, the garage was turned into a model workshop after a few years. The design studio was expanded by renting the first floor of one of the neighbouring houses from a widow. Several other garages housed drawing archives and models. When afternoon turned into evening and the young architects had left for the day, Jacobsen had his dinner served in the hall, which with its large ceramic floor tiles was like the house's piazza – or he ate outside in a suntrap in the garden. He could then use a large soft pencil to calmly explore all the sketches that were screaming for his amendments and comments ahead of another hectic day tomorrow.

One of Jacobsen's own photos of his garden with the many plants that he meticulously and lovingly tended to. Many of the plants can be recognised from his motifs for the textiles from the same period.

The *Ditch Edge* and *Forest Floor* patterns that Jacobsen had engrossed himself in and drawn as a textile during his exile in Sweden were now transformed into his own small miniature landscape when he began working on his garden in the early 1950s. It was a compact 300-square-metre plot and became an interaction between garden and textile pattern in such a way that the garden, when seen from the veranda on the first floor, became the textile *Skyview* – an abstract paraphrase of lines, circles, and asymmetrical patterns. Naturally, the garden didn't grow as quickly as the house itself but it nevertheless matured nicely over the years. Although it appeared green, it was half made of Norwegian Porsgrunn marble tiles, the same that Jacobsen used for the facades of his town and city halls in the 1930s and later the National Bank of Denmark. Maybe he had obtained them from one of his construction sites.

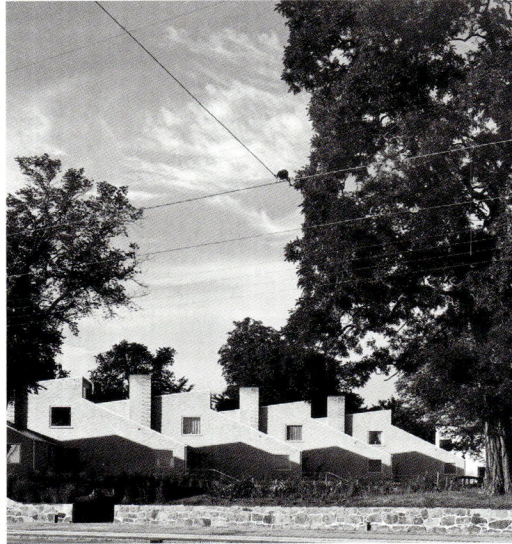

← Jacobsen's own house surrounded by large old trees. His own garden of less than 500 square metres extends to the left towards the busy Strandvej.

↓ Another view of the garden. Each plant exudes tranquillity, just like on the Swedish textiles. A gardener was hired to maintain the beautifully trimmed mini-hedges, as it was a garden that required a lot of upkeep.

→ Jacobsen's gardens are courtyards that can be transposed into framed pictures or textile patterns. His last were the sketches for the courtyards of the Danish National Bank. The motifs are well-known – green plants that neatly and aesthetically crawl outside of their beds.

The meticulous plan for Jacobsen's
garden with all the plants named – a
place for everything, and everything
in its place. The big white gap in the
middle is the house, and we can see
the large trees enrobing the entrance
on the left.

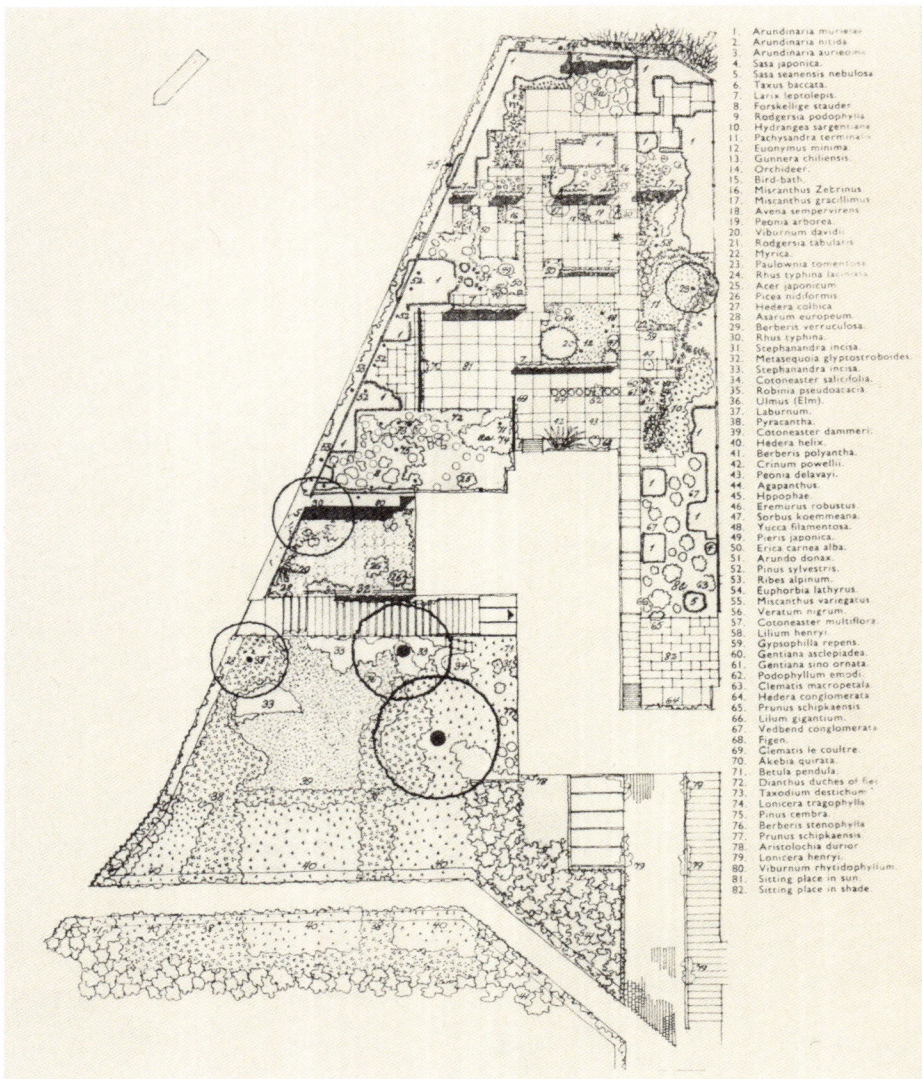

The garden plan is then translated into an abstract gouache, which probably served as the model for the slightly simpler abstract pattern *Skyview* for Grautex below. Whether the title refers to the view from his balcony on the first floor is anyone's guess.

The garden's perpendicular lines created an elegant and well-composed pattern. The paths formed a grid, where the narrow bushes helped to create partitions and backdrops down through the garden. In this way, the garden was a distinct spatial experience. The bushes were trimmed to be just 10 centimetres wide. It was a painstaking job to maintain. But that's how the garden was, like a finished layout for a textile. We can quite easily recognise the early textile motifs from Stockholm in it. It was understated, with lots of greenery, and maidenhair ferns between the thickets of bamboo. Deer ferns and sensitive ferns formed the finest evergreen carpets that seemingly thrived in this windswept garden, where the gusts off the Øresund did not make their survival easier. There were no large trees (stipulated by a covenant), a single empress tree with its small crown formed a perfect counterpoint, typical of Jacobsen. The predominantly green motifs, which also included narrow fields of grass, could be recognised in the more monochrome textiles. *Docks* or *Anemone* could be used as a tablecloth on the garden table and blended in so well that they could almost function as camouflage.

Heath pearlwort spilled over from the sides and colonised the joints and edges of the tiles. You had to tread carefully so as not to ruin the effect. Light and shadow, and not least the backlight, were clearly present in the composition. The garden faced south and looked most beautiful when viewed from the narrow veranda off the living room on the first floor. Like a captain on his bridge, Jacobsen would stand here and greet the passing beachgoers and enjoy his garden before disappearing into the basement to amend drawings.

There was a clear line between Dyrehaven and Gentofte that marked a no-man's land. The area around Gentofte had actually been a kind of military zone in the early 20th century. After the ramparts around inner Copenhagen fell 50 years earlier, construction began on a larger defensive ring around Greater Copenhagen in response to the much greater range of modern weapons. In the wedge between ancient forest and bog, the northern flank was lined with several concrete forts, equipped with cannons and flood systems, which could stop an army if necessary.

After the First World War, people realised that the defences were severely outdated. A tank could change position; a concrete fort could not. A bomb-laden warplane could easily fly over the flooded areas and reach the city. Accordingly, the idyllic area was demilitarised, and new residential neighbourhoods popped up on the outskirts of where royalty and merchants once lived.

The beautiful Jægersborg Allé with its castles ran through Gentofte. In the not-so-distant past, the Crown Prince and Princess had lived at Charlottenlund Castle by the Øresund, and European monarchs from Great Britain and Russia visited the royal family at Bernstorff Castle. At the very top, in Lyngby, we end up at Sorgenfri Castle, where members of the royal family also lived. The parallel road to this imposing avenue is called Soløsevej. It was not, as its Danish name might suggest, bathed in sun, as it was located in a forest surrounded by swampy meadows where pigs and sows could roam free. It was a poor area that bordered the forest. Just the place for the young and not yet well-versed architects who were hungry for

their own government-loan-funded house. They also wanted to build a modern home as a business card for their emerging design studio. Consequently, this road became a kind of architectural road, populated with great architects and furniture designers.

It stretched from the beach, with Jacobsen's terraced house in the front row, up to where his old school friend Mogens Lassen built functionalist houses, for which the old cannon towers were used to form a sturdy foundation. From there, it went on to Jacobsen's own first functionalist house from 1929 on Gotfred Rodes vej. Finn Juhl lived on the next side street, just a brick's throw away, and a little further from that were Jacobsen's good friends Nils and Eva Koppel. You also passed the houses of furniture connoisseurs Børge Mogensen and Hans Wegner. These are just some of the most famous names, but there were many others.

All of these homes could be found along the five-kilometre stretch and were also designed to serve as small business premises, with a design studio employing young architects at one end of the house, while the master architect and his family lived at the other. Small perhaps, but visionary. With modern furniture whose paint had barely dried, and with amenities such as central heating, American refrigerators, and flushing toilets. These modernities were still only available to a small number of the Danish population, who otherwise lived on a farm with an outhouse or in the city with a privy in the yard, and where the food was stored in a pantry, and not in a cold refrigerator with a freezer compartment.

Duck for Cotil, 1956. In the later years of Cotil, Arne and Jonna Jacobsen worked almost exclusively with abstract motifs. The motifs were either woven or printed.

The textile factory

Few of the other design studios were as multifaceted as Jacobsen's. His design studio rested on three distinct pillars. Architecture was the focal point and beating heart, and required the most effort. Then there was the furniture, lamps, and all the other interior design which, as the icing on the cake, filled the buildings and earnt money for the extra hours that Jacobsen spent on the architecture to make it truly sublime. In this regard, it was the two manufacturers, Fritz Hansen and Louis Poulsen, who were the primary partners, although several others were added from the late 1950s onwards. Finally, there were the textiles, which had provided Arne and Jonna with a financial safety net for almost a decade, starting with 14 textiles for Nordiska Kompaniet in 1944 to the many designs they now boasted. Unlike the furniture, far from all the motifs found their way into Jacobsen's buildings, because this part of the business was primarily a money-maker.

↑ *Park*. A textile with many producers: Nordiska Kompaniet, Almedahl, and Textil Lassen.

It is possibly from 1948. Note the small white park benches scattered around the motif.

↓ *Sea* for Textil Lassen, 1954. Made with four colours ranging from grey to blue. Arne and Jonna begin to move away from the deeply figurative motifs towards the more abstract. Here we're standing out in the water and looking down at the waves.

↑↓ *Rookery* for Grautex and Textil Lassen, 1954. Floral curtains in different colour schemes.

You can almost hear the quiet chattering of the birds in the dawn light.

→→ *Stalk* for Cotil. The same motif cycle as *Polygon* and *Duck*, playing with geometry and spaces. Kvadrat later produced it under the name *Angles*.

← *Forget-me-not* from
Grautex, here as a
wallpaper template.
Sample print showing
the rotation block being
repeated.

→ The textile *Water* has the
same motif cycle as *Sea* on
page 182, although a little
more naturalistic in the
colour scheme. Produced
for Textil Lassen.

↓ *Polygon* from Cotil, 1956,
later reissued by Georg
Jensen Damask. Similar
to *Duck* but only as a line
drawing.

Textiles had become a big business with a dozen manufacturers of upholstery fabrics, curtains, carpets, wallpapers, and even clothing textiles that needed to be catered for. And catering for them meant involved following up on existing patterns and developing new textiles, as well as adjusting the repeat, where the motif had to work in both directions. Then came fabric samples, weave densities and, not least, colour choices. There was plenty to decide on. This required a full-time employee, and it naturally fell

to Jonna. So while the basement was full of young architects and construction projects, Jonna sat in the upper rooms with the large arsenal of textiles, wallpapers, and patterns, negotiating with manufacturers.

Textiles and patterns were a playground for many artists and architects in the early 1950s. It was here that they could earn an extra penny or two. There were also plenty of wallpaper factories and textile manufacturers needing new designs who have long since disappeared.

Poul Gernes, Gunnar Aagaard Andersen, and not least the ubiquitous Verner Panton hopped on the bandwagon so zealously with their elegant and well-composed patterns that both Marie Gudme Leth and Jacobsen felt quite intimidated. But just like with the furniture and lamp manufacturers, there was an A and a B team. Those who knew how to keep up the pace, and those who didn't. Gunnar Aagaard Andersen and Verner Panton hedged their bets well with Percy von Halling-Koch's unique fabrics, as did Arne Jacobsen with Cotil.

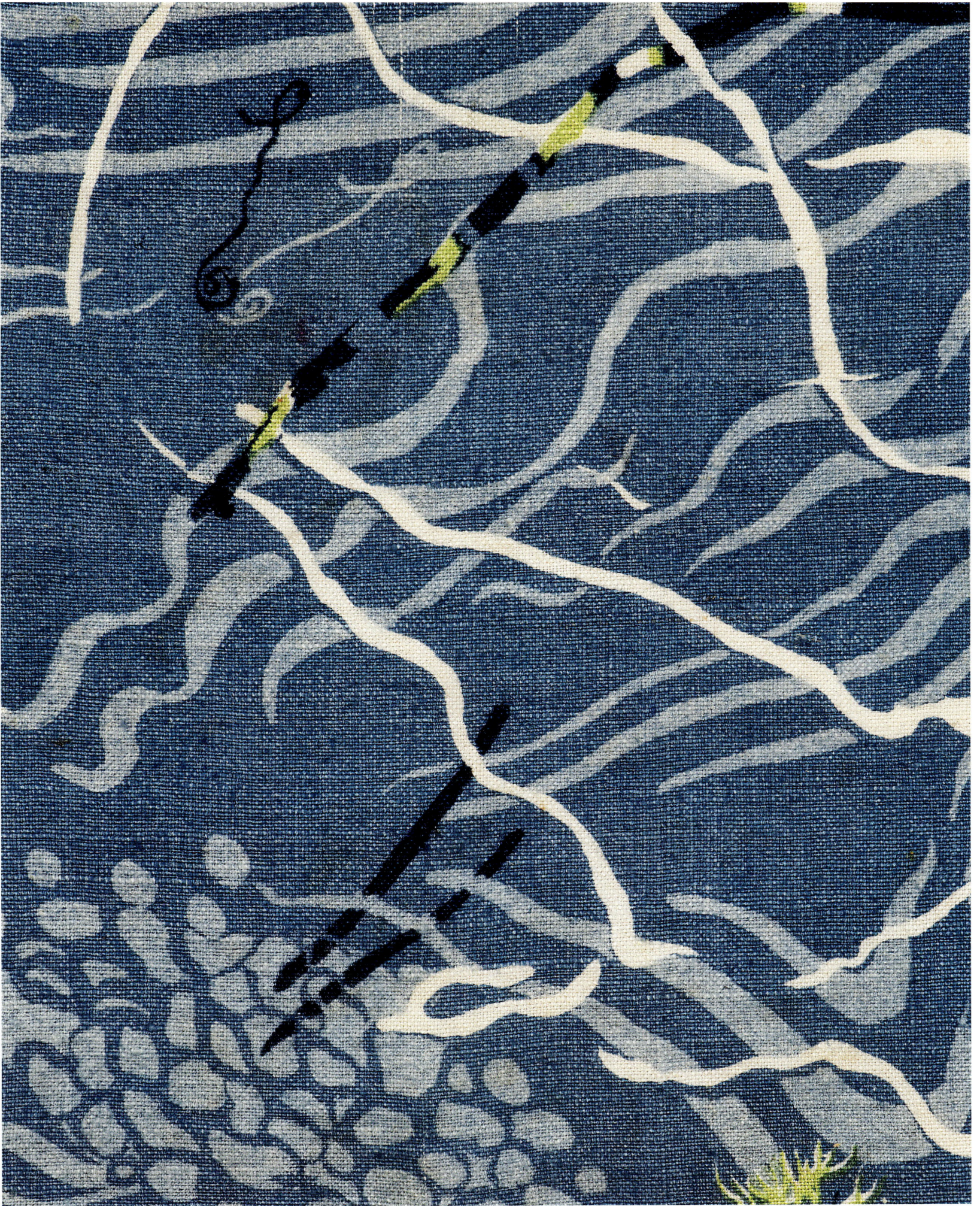

The naturalistic, the fun, and the abstract

At the beginning of the 1950s, the motifs of Jacobsen's textiles changed. It is no longer nature alone that is the main inspiration, but the abstract motifs created on a drawing board or on graph paper are also a significant influence. When Jacobsen introduced the *Scan-Am* furniture and the *Ant*, they were based on the abstract black and white *Trapez* pattern, among others. You can see traces of this even in his first textiles. First and foremost, the superior nature motifs such as the dramatic *Crown Imperial*, elegant Japanese calligraphy-inspired *Bamboo* and all the others that referenced familiar features of Sweden's nature such as *Forest Floor*, *Pond*, and *Ditch Edge*. But there had also been a more architect-friendly line with patterns like *Chain* and *Bio-Bio*, in addition to a relatively simple pattern like *Yes-No*, where daisies played tag.

Just before 1950, he designed a very commercial and quite humorous line, where clear domestic motifs interplayed with rhythm. Here we see *Hyacinth Glass*, *Lemons in Net*, *Cloche*, and the slightly Jacobsen-esque motif with motorways and airplanes that intertwine with each other. There's even a pattern with troops dropping from an airplane with white parachutes, perhaps landing in enemy territory. These are graphically beautiful motifs that were created straight on the drawing board, in contrast to the early motifs, where inspiration and execution were taken on a warm summer's day out in nature and then transformed into a pattern that could be repeated indefinitely when they were printed on reams of fabric in a machine production process.

Forest for Cotil. A number of motifs play with an abstract version of nature, almost like paper clippings. *Tassel* and *Pine* belong to the same family.

Hellebores for Cotil. Elegant motif in subdued colour compositions – a motif from Jacobsen's own garden.

Pine for Cotil. A motif from the abstract forest.

Ypsilon for Cotil. A textile with many different colour variations and a pattern that can work in many contexts.

In a survey from 1954, Jonna Jacobsen prepared a rough list of 32 textile motifs to be subject to negotiation with Textil-Lassen, who ultimately chose only nine patterns. The list included old motifs from 1943 and some slightly newer ones, clearly indicated by the number of printing frames needed to produce them. Some were printed simply and cheaply, like *Bio-Bio*, which had only a single printing frame, whereas *Reed* and *Hyacinth Glass* used as many as seven printing frames (or separate colours, in other words). During this period, the various textile companies also exchanged printing frames. Some patterns became unfashionable and were simplified with fewer colours to make them cheaper and more modern. Some of the companies also went bankrupt along the way and were taken over by others. Nordiska Kompaniet's printing films were transferred to Textil-Lassen and Grautex, but simplified versions of them were later put into production at Cotil. The same printing film was also used as a template for wallpapers for Tapettrykkeriet, Dansk Tapetfabrik, Grautex, and Brdr. Dahls Tapetfabrik. On the side of the textile or wallpaper, there was often, but not always, text like: COLLIERE comp by ARNE JACOBSEN a GRAUTEX fabric.

Jacobsen's preferred manufacturer from the mid-1950s would come to be the textile company C. Olesen with the Cotil brand. They had a desire to raise the standard of home textiles. The advertisements read: "Home textiles, designed and coloured by Nordic artists. Selected and approved by an independent committee." The 1953 committee included Mogens Koch, Børge Mogensen, and Lis Ahlmann, who also drew patterns for the collection, so you can judge their independence for yourselves. In any case, the Jacobsens submitted several designs that were accepted.

The work process was changed during these years. Professional fabric pens, felt-tip pens, and geometric guides replaced the large Jacobsen-esque watercolour brush. There are countless prototypes from this time. Sketches that bear witness to repetition upon repetition before arriving at a very precise pattern. Rectangular patterns and circles are the recurring motif. *Ypsilon*, *Vertigo*, and *Angles* are some of the entirely abstract motifs, while patterns such as *Pine* and *Fir* represent an abstract, yet recognisable form of nature. In addition, a number of older naturalistic models were edited and modernised. Around 20 printed textiles were developed in this way, peaking at the end of the 1950s. Added to that were the woven textiles with all their colour variations.

Arne and Jonna worked with Kirsten and John Becker's hand-weavery on a wide range of projects. Unique woven textiles were produced here, including curtains. The large stage and backdrop from Munkegård school was made at the weaving mill in Søllerød. A few years later, prototypes of bedspreads and curtains were made for the Royal Hotel.

Since the early 1940s, Jacobsen had painted nature both intensely and precisely. He did not temper the explosive colour palette of his naturalistic motifs. After all, when depicting a ditch edge or a summer meadow, colour is unavoidable. In motifs like *Crown Imperial*, the red of the plant stands out against the green of the leaves. Although the motif contained many colour nuances, it was the red against the green that held the motif together. It was the complementary colours that made the design resonate so intensely. In other cases, his textiles were sometimes much more muted, with blue flowers and blue-green leaves. He was a skilled colourist and knew what he could achieve with colours.

An example of Jacobsen's approach to colours can be seen in his Royal Hotel. Here, the horizontal building block is in blue-green metal sheets, while the core tower, which rises vertically from the horizontal block, has ice-green glass sheets that complement the changing sky, from bright blue to dark graphite grey. Inside, the hotel is dressed in muted colours, such as the wenge wood panels with their deep reddish-brown grain that serve to bring nature inside. This in turn stands out against the British racing green. The furniture created for the hotel – the *Egg*, the *Swan*, the *Drop*, and all the other famous chairs – stood as stark accents against the subdued interior. Woollen shades in light green and light blue contrasted with the elegant dark blue uniforms of the SAS flight attendants – this was, after all, an international airline hotel owned by SAS.

The shell chairs, lamps, and textiles all had a full-scale yet toned-down palette, going from rusty red through shades of grass green towards blue, deep brown, and black. Yet another palette was developed by Jacobsen for the textile company Cotil. These textiles were no longer intended for his own houses, but for private homes. These were adapted to a market and a time when muted colours were fashionable. The woven fabrics from Cotil were usually solid colours that could be mixed with each other. Although attempts were made with more everyday textiles inspired by Lis Ahlmann's work, it seems that it is the more lively and modern woven textile *Rain* that became the preferred upholstery for the furniture at the Royal Hotel.

One of the more unknown genres that Jacobsen worked in was tapestries. For example, he designed a large rug for the council chamber of Aarhus City Hall, as well as a smaller rug showing the floor plan of the city hall itself for the mayor's office. Both rugs were created with a flat-woven technique called flossa. A few years later, Jacobsen created another tapestry for an exhibition promoting handicrafts in the Netherlands in 1947. It was an extremely charming motif, perhaps from his beloved Bellevue. It is a ground plan with three bare trees in a lawn with a stone outcrop and three trunks protruding into the water. It was colourful, with shades of green and blue.

In 1957, Jacobsen won first and third prize in a carpet competition for the department store Magasin du Nord. Both proposals went into production. A third design was added the following year when Magasin du Nord transferred its carpet business to Gram Tæpper. Motifs such as *Staffs*, *Rings*, and *Lines* serve as a discreet foundation for the complete staging of Jacobsen's interiors. These were latecomers to Jacobsen's foray into tapestries.

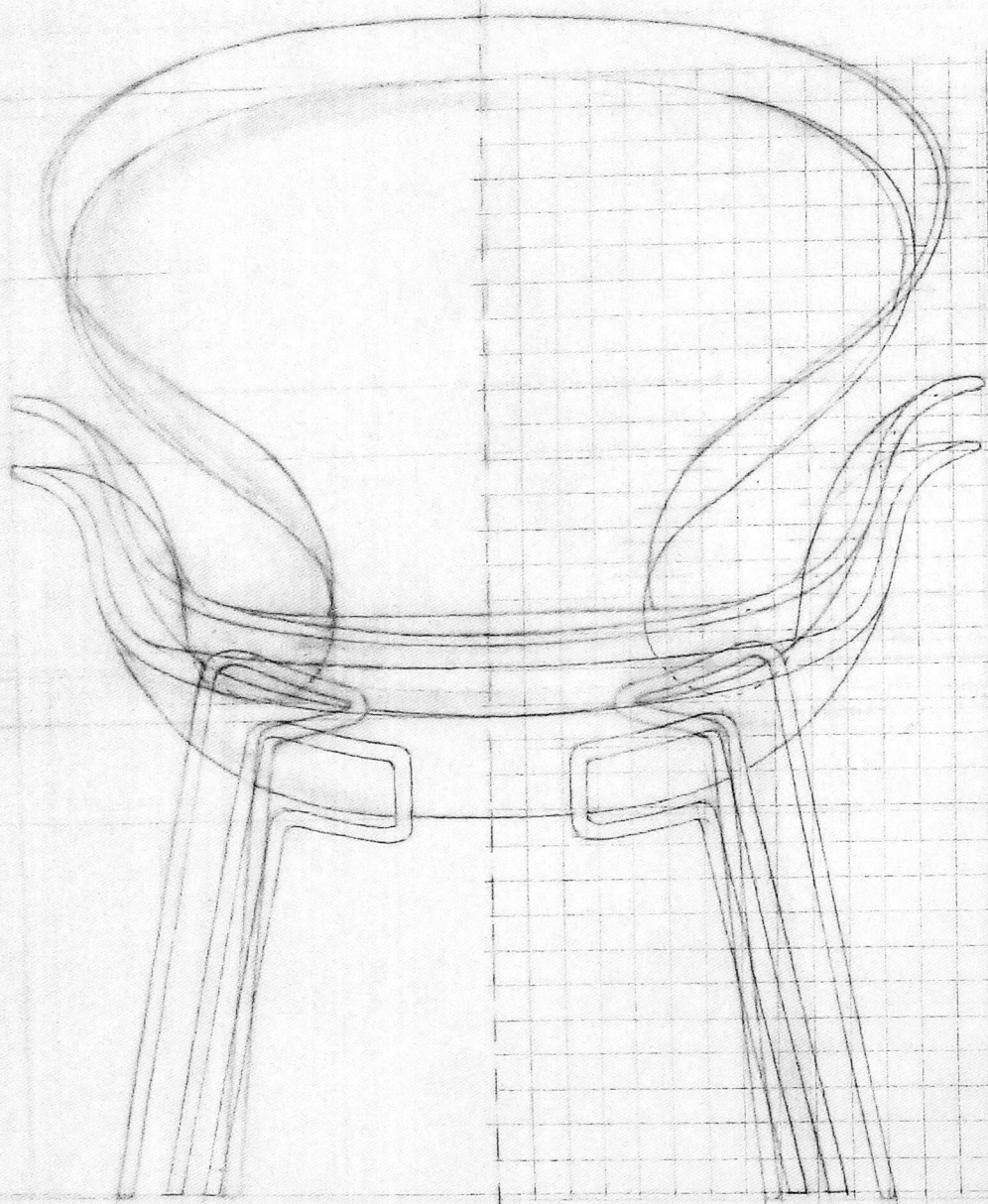

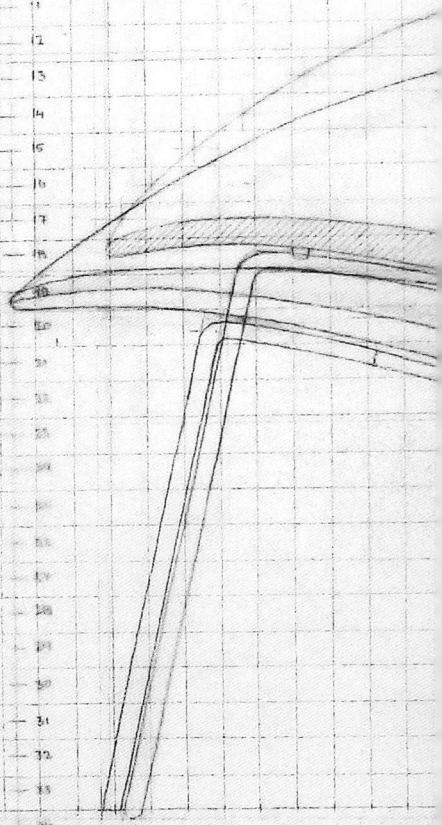

STOL SET FORFRA.

SNIT I MIDTERLINIE.
SIDEBILLEDE.

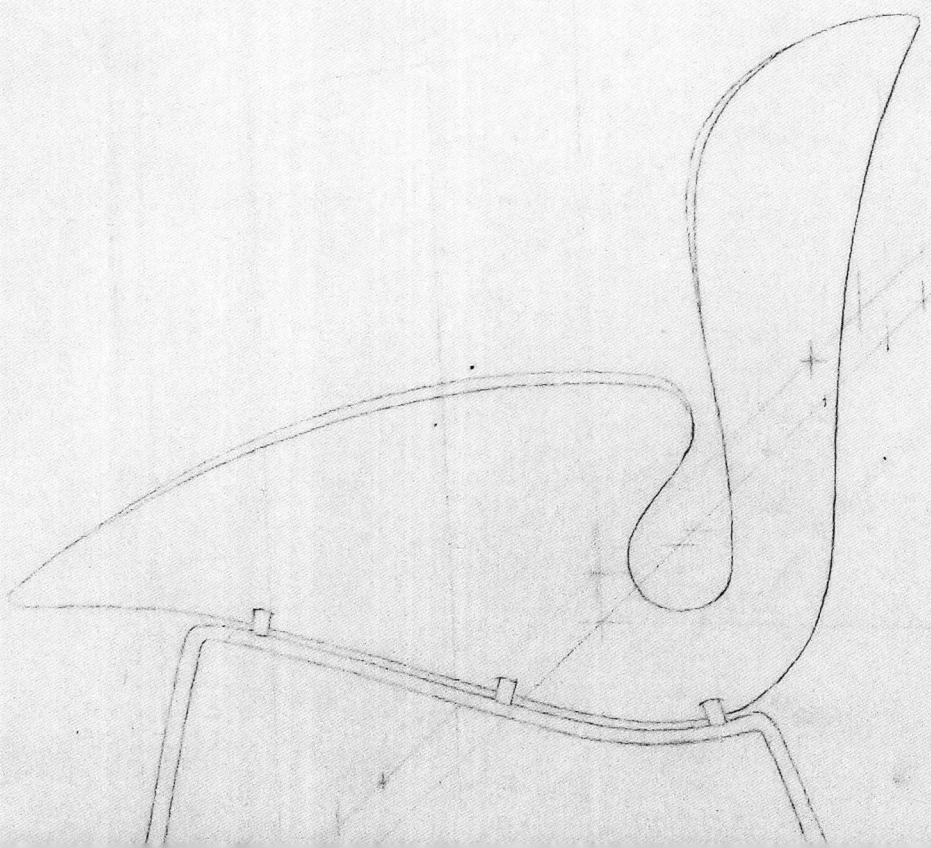

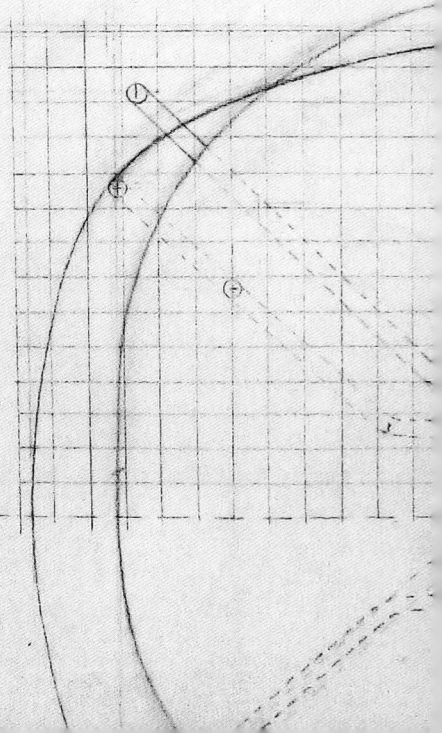

Some time before the Royal Hotel became a reality, development work had begun on what would become the *Swan*. It started as a laminated shell chair on a tubular steel frame and became more refined with each step. When it transpired that it was impossible to bend the plywood that much, the project evolved towards the foamed upholstered chair we know today.

Nevertheless, the *Ant* can still be recognised as a motif in the design. Here we see two sets of sketches superimposed on each other. The *Swan* as both a reclining lounge chair and as a regular dining chair in thin, bare plastic. The end result ended up having foam padding, probably made of fibreglass.

→ A working drawing of the *Swan*, showing the complicated curve. Jacobsen once explained on television that the design studio had to model the chair in chicken wire and plaster, as it was completely impossible to draw such a curved shape. Only when the plaster model was complete and approved could the necessary drawings be prepared, which is what we see here.

↓ The final design of the *Swan*, upholstered here in fabric and mounted on a swivel base. The model shown is an early version, where the cast aluminium base consists only of the cross itself on the floor, a bit like a Christmas tree base. The rotating cylinder is also mounted into a round hole in the base. In the original first edition, the cylinder was somewhat larger, like a column growing out from the bottom, cast in the same process as the rest of the base.

↑ A small cardboard scale model of the *Swan*. Here it was probably intended as a shell chair, probably made of laminated veneer and with a tubular frame that is quite similar to the *Series 7*, only lower.

Here we can see the *Swan* at Rødovre Library, which was designed by Jacobsen's design studio and built in the early 1960s. Between the two chairs is a small side table, which was part of the same furniture series. On the wall, the *AJ Lamp* is mounted so that it shines downwards. Mounted in this way, it is also known by the nickname *Pixie*.

In the mid-1950s, Norwegian furniture and interior designer Henry W. Klein, together with two technicians from a small furniture factory in Kristiansand in Norway succeeded in stabilising the foam material polystyrene – what most people know as Styrofoam. It was now possible to make a stable, hard shell that could be upholstered, just like other furniture designs. He was inspired by his teacher Finn Juhl, who had good contacts in the US and could discuss the new wonder material, polystyrene. However, it was too soft to hold its shape on its own, and so the idea of making furniture out of it was abandoned at Finn Juhl's design studio, where Henry Klein worked for a time.

After many attempts, Henry Klein and his team in Kristiansand finally solved the riddle. They applied for a patent, sketched several furniture proposals in the material, and planned a tour of Scandinavia. In 1956, Klein visited Fritz Hansen and met with the Hansen brothers. They bought the patent, but not his furniture proposal. He had a quirky and simple idea for a chair to take around on his tour. An armchair shaped like an egg and set on a swivel base. He had earmarked it for Bramin Møbelfabrik the following year, where he was also employed as design manager. He also sold his polystyrene patent to about 45 other factories, and now foamed plastic chairs were popping up everywhere.

Klein should have been happy and proud, but something came to haunt him for the rest of his life. He thought he was the father of the *Egg*. Bramin's Egg wasn't a success and was overtaken by Finnish interior designer Eero Aarnio's Egg, which clearly depicted a perfectly sliced egg. However, Klein was redressed by allying himself with Jørn Utzon, who had returned home in frustration after things broke down with the City of Sydney. Together they developed the somewhat strange modular chair system *Utsep*, made of polystyrene.

Meanwhile, Jacobsen had started developing a lounge chair based on the *Ant* – an oval-shaped back with a seat curved into a bowl shape, giving the chair armrests. The first attempts were made as a veneer shell similar to his other shell chairs, but the shape wouldn't really work because the trestles were too strong and the chair was too clumsy.

It took two lucky coincidences before Jacobsen managed to hatch his own egg. In 1956, his design studio was working on the initial sketches for a hotel for SAS, which was to become Denmark's first skyscraper. He wanted to furnish this building with his own furniture, but up to this point, he had only designed functional chairs and little by way of useful or attractive armchairs. Søren Hansen then showed him the patent and sketches from Henry Klein, which got Jacobsen thinking.

He was given free rein to make his lounge furniture, which could then be used in the hotel ... at least initially. It was a smart idea, because the development costs could then be covered by purchases for the hotel.

However, it didn't stop at just one chair. By 1958, the series had been developed into five foam-covered chairs using the new technology. They were quite formal chairs without much padding, with only the hard fabric-covered polystyrene as a seating surface.

The design studio had tried to further develop the *Swan* from the *Ant*, but it was difficult to achieve with a laminated veneer shell. Yet the improved polystyrene material paved the way for bold new possibilities. The *Ant* or the future *Swan* was sketched out, not only as an upholstered lounge chair, but also as a bare dining chair. However, in 1958, the technology wasn't quite advanced enough for this, and so it fell to the upholstered lounge chair. The flimsy frame was used instead for the *Pot* chair.

But the *Swan* soon found its final form as a foam-covered, upholstered lounge chair made of polystyrene. It was placed in the hotel's rooms, offices, and hallways – also in an extended version as a sofa, with a foam centre piece inserted very pragmatically into the basic shape of a *Swan* chair.

The original *Drop* chair placed where it was intended – in front of the dressing tables in the rooms of the SAS Royal Hotel. The *Drop* was made in the same way as the *Swan* and the *Egg* in a foam plastic material and then upholstered in either fabric or leather. At the time, production was limited to roughly the number needed for the hotel. Many years later, it has come back into production, now in hard plastic.

The original *Tongue* with its sputnik legs was also reshaped into a foam-covered chair and given an egg-shaped base and an exaggerated pointed back. It was named the *Drop* and became the primary piece of furniture at the small, elegant café Snackbaren, which connected the hotel lobby with the departure hall. It was also used in the rooms as the standard chair at the dressing table. The teardrop shape was repeated in the tabletop series that was designed for the table setting in the restaurant, and which jeweller A. Michelsen produced in silverplating along with the cutlery for the restaurant.

The *Pot* was an original piece not based on a previous model. Fritz Hansen maybe hoped that it would be this chair that would become the big bestseller, since it was both refined and yet also quite pared back. The thin *Series 7* frame, originally intended for the *Swan*, was placed on the *Pot*, which was then also upholstered. It adorned the hotel's elegant orchid garden, which took the form of a glass case in the corner behind the wide staircase, allowing light to seep into the lobby, Snackbaren café, and the bar on the first floor. In one of the bars, the *Pot* even appeared as a wall-mounted sofa, several metres long. This was a pragmatic solution achievable thanks to the polystyrene construction which could be sawn to shape and planed to insert a centre piece of the desired length.

↓ This chair was called the *Pot*, and it was made in the same way as the other foam chairs. It was a variant of the original *Swan* sketches on page 203. It did not have the *Swan*'s wings, but was made with the slender steel tube frame as in the first sketches.

→ Japanese women in kimonos admire the hanging orchids, which are delicately hung inside the double glass wall of the orchid garden. It was an oasis where coffee and tea were served to people enjoying the *Pot* chairs. One of Jacobsen's 'large' rooms, which no longer exists. The room was a large glass box that cut through the low wing of the hotel and let in daylight from above. In this way, Jacobsen could play with the interaction between plants and light. It served to break the reception from the Snackbaren café and provided light to the rooms. Now the entire basement of the Royal Hotel lies in gloom and darkness.

The *Giraffe* chair. This page shows an early version that has survived in storage for many years. It is without the wooden mouldings that the final version had, which can be seen at the top-right on the opposite page. It was the one that was used in the hotel restaurant, among other places, as seen in the photo at the bottom-right. Up in the round skylights you can make out the glass bells, which were lit when darkness fell.

The *Giraffe* was a curiously hybrid chair. Its interior was a polystyrene shell that was upholstered in light green and framed with strips of ash wood. It was a pastiche that perhaps went well with the blue-painted tableware in the restaurant which had been painted with slightly unconventional, light green flowers to match the chair.

The *Giraffe*, on the other hand, was a bastard of a chair. In its basic form, it was perhaps an attempt at a multi-purpose chair with a high or low back. Producing the low version was easy, because the factory could simply cut the top of the polystyrene on the high version with a saw, thereby creating the low version. And then it all went completely wrong. Thin ash wood slats were mounted at the transition between the back and front of the chair to provide an edge for the upholstery. And in a special edition, the sides were also cut off to be replaced by an elaborately designed side that was a bit reminiscent of an airplane seat armrest.

The frame was designed with teak legs that were first bent and later milled into a T-shaped profile and assembled into a cross under the seat. This solution was adopted from the *Grand Prix* chair from 1957. The *Giraffe*, named after its somewhat unfortunate lumpy appearance, could be found in the large restaurant on the first floor of the SAS hotel and in the director's office. It was probably the most experimental chair and perhaps an attempt to find out how far one could go in combining modern plastic with the more traditional wood.

↓ A watercolour from around 1950 of a proposal for a development at Skovshoved harbour. Although it's not the *Egg* depicted in the bottom-left corner – that was first

modelled in plaster about seven years later – the drawing clearly shows that Jacobsen had early ideas about upholstered chairs in a new organic design language.

→ The armchair that came to be called the *Egg* was also embedded into the concept of the Royal Hotel, both in the rooms, as seen below, and in the lobby.

The *Egg* is upholstered in black leather and has the original base, which is die-cast in one piece of aluminium. The *Egg*, the *Drop*, and all the

tabletops in the hotel had their origins in an organic design language that, to some extent, alludes to chicken eggs.

The largest of the shell chairs was the *Egg*, with its external appearance resembling a giant egg, in which an incision has been made, making it somewhat reminiscent of the classic ear-flap chair with 'ears' that the user could lean their head against. There were some narrow and modest armrests that could then guide the body down into the shell. The seat cushion is a later addition, as criticism rained down on the chair, with accusations that the polystyrene was too hard to sit on.

The *Egg* was used in the large foyer, enabling guests to hide while they watched what was going on around them. And with a little push of your foot you could turn the chair and swivel away from prying eyes. Welcome to the informal 1960s and the decade of playful furniture.

Henry Klein's *Egg* for Bramin came on the market at the same time as Jacobsen's *Egg*, but it was Jacobsen who triumphed and was proclaimed to have created an unforgettable design icon. He was inspired by the best and so optimised the design to the fullest. With his excellent eye, he could take a design that seemed finished and then add – or rather pare back – and make it his own.

The *Series 7* similarly adopted the back from the *Dan* chair. And on a grand scale, the SAS hotel's basic concept was created with clear references to Lever House in New York, designed by the architectural firm Skidmore, Owings & Merrill and inaugurated in 1952. Rødovre Town Hall demonstrated very clear features from Eero Saarinen's General Motors Styling Center in Detroit. It was also from here that the central spiral staircase in Jacobsen's foyer in the SAS Royal Hotel borrowed much of its distinctive character. And finally, Jacobsen continued Eero Saarinen's idea of placing organic plastic chairs in the sharply cut glass cases, which Jacobsen brilliantly carried over into the SAS Royal Hotel.

The Royal Hotel was a large project, handled by an architectural firm that was still quite small at the time. The hotel was designed right down to the smallest detail, with shops, graphics, textiles, and furniture. The five shell chairs alone must have required an immense amount of resources to design and develop for production. The line was drawn from the start – that is, the characteristic the contour line. It was the line that, from the *Ant* onwards created the easily recognisable chair shells, and which was continued here in the *Egg* in the form of the stitching that divides the front and back of the chair. This abrupt line, like a thick contour line in a comic book, completes the shape and creates distance from the surroundings.

Rødovre Town Hall was designed and built between 1954 and 1956. Jacobsen's focus on details that bear the hallmarks of industrial manu-facturing becomes increasingly evident in this period. Here we can see a section of the main staircase inside the building.

The creation process behind the foam chairs and sofas was simpler than for the plywood shell chairs. Working drawings with cross-sections and outlines were made in full scale and helped to serve as the basis for production. The proportions were tested in plaster, and the negative shapes were given equal consideration as the positive ones when evaluating the final design. When the outline of the furniture, the contour, is so important, you also have to look at what's 'missing' in the shape and in the surrounding space. It's similar to the drawing of fonts – the white paper around the black letter is just as important as the shape of the letter itself. Comfort could also be carefully tested in the plaster model. The *Egg* was first found to be too narrow, after which it was resolutely cut lengthwise and made wider. When the final model was complete and approved, a cast of the plaster mould could be made, just like when a classical sculpture was cast. This casting was used as the starting point for the final aluminium casting tools from which the polystyrene shell could be cast, including the narrow steel rod with bushings that would be used to mount the base.

The foyer of the town hall, like the rest of the building, is furnished and equipped with Jacobsen's own designs. Here, for example, we can see a 3303 sofa with accompanying table, and a *Munkegård Lamp* hanging from the ceiling.

Details from the council chamber at Rødovre Town Hall. The clock is a variant of the clocks that were designed for Aarhus City Hall and Søllerød Town Hall, but the dial is in a lighter colour. The up-light system was specially designed for this location.

→ Ashtrays were integrated into all the tables in the council chamber. They can be flipped out completely or pushed in so that they're almost invisible.

Once Jacobsen was completely satisfied, he moved on to upholstered prototypes, where the stitching created a defining line between the front and back. That was the case with the textile version – in the leather version, a thin leather ridge helped to define the join. Finally, full-scale working drawings were made with cross-sections and outlines. With these, the basis for production was complete to enable a cast of the plaster mould for the finished model to be made, just like when a classical sculpture is cast. This casting was used as the starting point for the final aluminium tools from which the polystyrene shell could be cast, including the narrow steel rod with bushings at the bottom that would be used to mount the base.

The main entrance to Rødovre Town Hall is a minimalist hi-tech design, heavily inspired by General Motors' design centre in Detroit, which was designed by Finnish architect Eero Saarinen. The *Munkegård Lamps* are used in many places at the town hall, including under the large half-roof.

→ → The council chamber in a rather cool modernist style with marble floors, a futuristic lighting system, and furniture in the refined and simplified style of the time. The chairs must have been added later, because the *Oxford* chair was first designed for St Catherine's College some five to seven years later.

Once you find a winning formula, you must use it. That seems to have been Jacobsen's design philosophy in the 1950s. With the shell chairs, the formula was simple – it was the contour that drew the seat shell and gave it life and beauty. Jacobsen applied this method to cutlery, a door handle, and an exhibition pavilion.

During the design and fitting out of the Royal Hotel, Jacobsen was tasked with designing a proposal for in-flight cutlery for SAS's transatlantic flights. This refined cutlery was useful on a plane where there wasn't much elbow room. However, the design was not used. Instead, it was Sigvard Bernadotte's design that won, while Finn Juhl was tasked with designing the interiors of SAS's offices around the world, so Jacobsen was out of that job, too.

But in connection with the hotel, Jacobsen entered into a collaboration with court jeweller and silversmith A. Michelsen to create new cutlery for the hotel's dining areas – the restaurant, café, and room service. He further developed the rejected SAS cutlery design, now in silverplating. The cutlery was made longer and more slender and was now produced in the classic way – cast in brass and then silver-plated and stamped with the iconic two towers stamp found on cutlery across Denmark. It was named *AJA*, but Jacobsen received complaints that it was too flimsy and that you couldn't get a pea up to your mouth using the fork. This simply wouldn't do at an international restaurant with a view of Tivoli in a country like Denmark, which also has a national poet who has written a fairy tale about the princess and the pea. The cutlery was taken back and continued in small production runs for a while afterwards. Among other things it was later used in St Catherine's College at the professors' high table.

However, Jacobsen and his new manufacturer A. Michelsen got along well and agreed to make a cheap mass-produced set of cutlery,

the *AJ cutlery*, making it the third cutlery set that Jacobsen designed within a very short period of time.

This new set of utensils was even more flimsy than the previous ones, and it was even more impossible for a pea to balance on its journey from the plate to the mouth. All the parts were made from flat steel that was punched and pressed into shape and then brushed. This created a certain familiarity between the individual parts, which was further reinforced by the intentional narrowness of the cutlery's dimensions. It was very modern, minimalist, and artistically advanced. The knife looks like something from an operating table, where the blade and handle merge into one, and the fork only has three blunt tips, the norm being four. Finally, there is the spoon, which is so narrow that it cannot hold much liquid, and therefore a special soup spoon was designed where the spoon bowl (the depression in the spoon from which you eat) sits on the side of the handle and not at the end. And of course it had to come in two versions – one for right-handed people and one for left-handed people.

The cutlery had a strangely coherent form, even though it might seem difficult to fathom, considering the odd flat parts. Jacobsen had used his winning formula – it was the outline, the so-called contour line, that gave the shape. The *AJ cutlery* was a fairly extensive set of cutlery with many sizes ranging from teaspoons to salad servers, but everything had the same basic shape. In addition, a smaller lunch cutlery set was made to complement the larger dinner cutlery. The *AJ cutlery* was also featured as the cutlery of the future in Stanley Kubrick's science fiction film "2001: A Space Odyssey" from 1968. The pea here turned into a green puree that could be quickly devoured with an AJ spoon by the lonely astronaut Dave, who eventually has to fight the demonic computer HAL.

After several unsuccessful attempts, Jacobsen hit the spot with his stainless steel cutlery.
For the Royal Hotel, he designed the more ordinary silver plated

AJA cutlery and also developed a proposal for in-flight cutlery for SAS, which never went into production.
He subsequently created the iconic AJ cutlery for A.

Michelsen. Ultra-narrow spoons and forks that could barely hold a pea. A knife that would look just as at home on an operating table as in the cutlery drawer.

And finally, an asymmetrical soup spoon, which came in both a right-handed and left-handed version.
The parts came together as a whole and fit together

beautifully. The secret, as always, was the master's conviction in proportions and his contour line. This is the same type of line as on the shell chairs, where the seam between the

front and back moulds and defines the shape. If you want to be a real geek, hold the fork against the tall Oxford chair – it's the same shape.

A wide range of fixtures had been developed for the town and city halls, which were designed from the late 1930s into the early 1940s, with the door handle for Søllerød Town Hall in particular exuding great strength and power. But in the 1950s, a new handle had to be created. What would it look like if you took a *Swan* or an *Egg* and morphed them into a door handle instead? That could well have been Jacobsen's starting point. It is said that he squeezed a lump of window putty with his hand and very specifically showed how to grip a door handle. A large curved surface on the handle accommodates the hollowness of the hand, and the thumb naturally slides onto the slightly hollow concave curve, which matches the turning movement of the wrist when the door handle is pushed downwards. With the winning formula from the shell chair's contour line in mind, the handle could be designed. That is to say, the tightness of the contour line gives the sculptural shape and the curved line between the top and bottom.

↓ The *AJ* door handle in the original version made of brass and well-patinated. This design is crafted to fit well into the hollow of the hand, and there is a nice space for the thumb to rest on.

→ The candlesticks in the table-top series used in the Royal Hotel's restaurant and café area. Most of this product line did not go beyond hotel use, but the heavy silver-plated candlesticks did make their way to retail. Originally made by court jeweller A. Michelsen and later produced by Georg Jensen.

The oval-egg influence

What Jacobsen tried to do throughout the 1950s was to anchor his design through a few aesthetic laws and key principles. The contour lines on the shell chairs were one example, the egg-shaped chair was another, and later in the 1960s the cylinder was used for many purposes. The egg shape played a key role in one series of Jacobsen's objects. The lounge chair the *Egg* is of course included in this category, and so is the *Drop*. But this shape also appeared in the restaurants. Along with his first set of cutlery, Jacobsen made a series of tableware for the restaurants and cafés in the SAS hotel. All with the ball shape and the egg as the main motif.

It was also at A. Michelsen's silversmith works that the turned brass pieces were soldered together and then silver-plated. The somewhat ordinary glasses that Jacobsen and his employees designed, and which were produced by Kastrup Glasværk, also contained some of the shapes from this theme. Although there were many topics that emerged from this form, it seemed as if no convincing kinship was forged between them. While one could say that the slightly awkward items in the *AJ cutlery* set end up complementing each other, that is not the case here. This series of table-top designs was quickly forgotten again. The only object that survived was the massive candlestick consisting of three balls and tall, slender candles.

↓ Sketch for the drinking glass series that Jacobsen designed for the Royal Hotel. The design is characterised by lively S-shaped curves that reflect the egg-shaped salt and pepper sets on the tables.

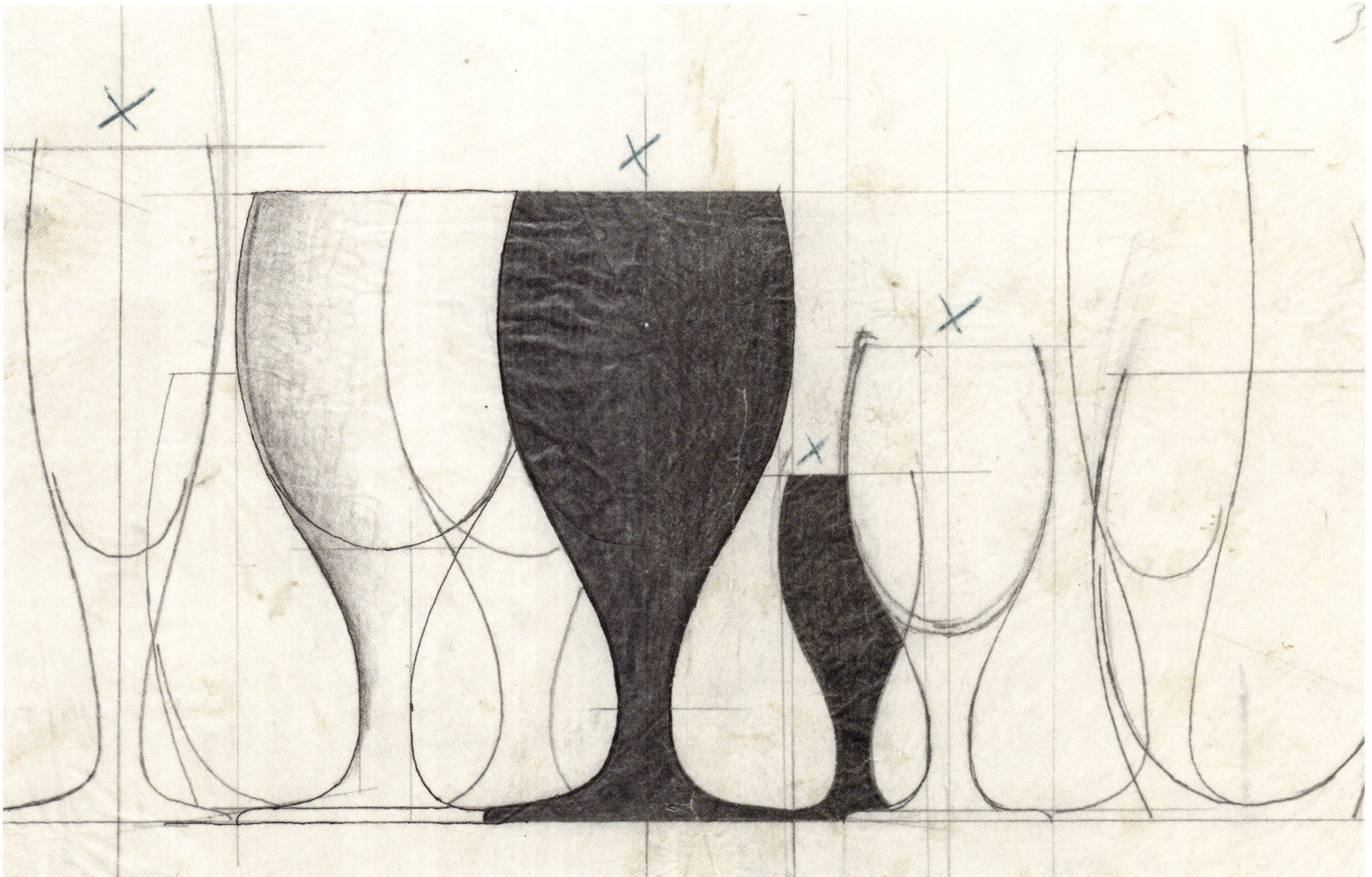

↑ The finished glass series, which was largely only used in the hotel as it was not distinctive enough to survive on the open market. With Royal Hotel, Jacobsen began collaborating with new manufacturers. Lyngby Copenhagen produced flat ashtrays, A. Michelsen manufactured silver-plated cutlery and table-top wares, and Kastrup Glasværk received the order for glass. The glass domes used in the cumbersome bell lamp in the restaurant, and which hung like clusters in the round skylights, came from Björkshult in Sweden.

↓ Plat-de-ménage for serving at the SAS hotel, salt and pepper shakers, and a mustard jar. Made of two brass parts that are soldered together and then polished and silver-plated.

The wall version of the
AJ Lamp, which shines
downwards on the phone
book shelf in the foyer of
the Royal Hotel. The first
version of the *AJ Lamp* was
this wall-mounted version.
Only later were the floor
lamp and table lamp
models drawn.

The post-war evolution of Jacobsen's design language, which took a major step forwards with the *Ant*, was also reflected in his and the design studio's work with the various lamp solutions of the decade. Like today, there were two main types of lighting – lamps primarily aimed at the private environment, and lamps especially intended for the public environment. The boundary between these two categories is, of course, blurred. For example, a hotel with a lobby, restaurant, and rooms serves as both a public area and a private space. Similarly, built-in ceiling fixtures and fixed wall lights can, in some cases, find their way into private homes. Jacobsen's most well-known lamp designs can be found in private and semi-private environments in particular.

It was primarily his work on the SAS hotel, and not least the interior design of the rooms and lounge areas, that prompted the development of the new lamps. The most widespread is the series with the common name the *AJ Lamp*. It was designed as a freestanding table lamp, a floor lamp, and a fixed wall fixture. The cylindrical lamp housing itself as well as the funnel-shaped shade are the common motif in the series. There is something geometrically strict about this design, such as the straight line that runs the length of the cylinder to the top edge of the shade.

The rather abrupt edge at the end of the lamp housing's cylinder also contributes to this sense of formal precision. On the other hand, the foot deviates slightly from the pure geometric look. It is a flat, egg-shaped profile with a large circular hole, which, if you look a little closer, seems to correspond nicely with precision of the shade's circular opening. An extremely thin metal tube only 10 mm in diameter connects the two elements. This seems especially delicate on the floor lamp model, in the same vein as the thin seat shells and legs on the *Ant* and the *Series 7*.

Several variants either existed from the off or were launched over the years after the design was finalised in 1957. The first lamps in the series were the wall-mounted versions, with the up-light version believed to be the original model from which the others were developed. The wall version also came in several sizes – either for fixing to the wall above an electrical outlet, or with a cord and its own push-button switch on the base. Turned downwards, the *AJ Lamp* could be used as a reading lamp or bedside lamp, to name just a few examples of its applications. The table lamp was available in two sizes, and all models were available in several colours starting with light grey, black, or dark brown, and later expanding to more colours depending on what the manufacturer Louis Poulsen thought was marketable at the time.

In 1958, the *AJ Pendant* became the next lamp for the SAS hotel, designed by Jacobsen and the design studio. It was, as the name suggests, a ceiling-hung lamp that initially only came in one, relatively large, version. The shape was a half sphere with a diameter of 50 cm, so like the *AJ Lamp*, it was a design with roots in geometry. Later it also came in a 37 cm version. The original version for the hotel was made of copper and brass, but was subsequently produced in lacquered versions in black, light grey, and brown. From the outset, the interior construction was more complicated than the formal geometric exterior indicates. There was a smaller inner shade, also hemi-spherical, which both provided reflected light and separated two different light sources. Mounted pointing vertically downwards in the inner shade was a powerful top-mirrored bulb. Meanwhile at the top of the fixture, there were three smaller bulbs between the two shades. These two different light sources could be turned on separately or together, so there was a choice between three different brightness levels and an equal number of lighting options. In later versions of the small *AJ Pendant*, the lighting was reduced to a single 100 W incandescent bulb.

At the top of the large outer shade were six lamellar-shaped openings that followed the spherical shape all the way around. These provided ventilation for the substantial amount of heat generated from up to four bulbs, and also provided a bit of upward general lighting. In a way, it was Poul Henning-sen's lighting system that quietly put its head above the parapet here. One of his smart ideas was that a pendant lamp hanging over a dining table, for example, should also provide light upwards and to the sides, so that the primary downward light would not become too glaring, and the shadows too dark and menacing. The *AJ Pendant* was used, among other places, in the SAS hotel lounge areas and later in the canteen in the National Bank of Denmark.

Alongside the two high-profile lighting designs, the design studio created a few lesser-known lamps. One is called *AJ-Royal* and is a floor lamp from 1958, which gives off a more general and diffused light. The shade is a milky white plastic tube with an oval profile and covered with an off-white textile. The metal frame consists of a base and a vertical rod, both either lacquered grey or brown. *AJ-Royal* was typically used in the hotel rooms and lobby. The second lamp is from 1959 and is called *Royal Pendant*. It was used in the Snackbaren café in the SAS hotel and was extremely simple, consisting of just four smoke-coloured acrylic sheets pressed into each other using slots milled into the sheets. This simple hanging lamp was shaped like a cube, measuring 21 cm on all sides. A 60 W carbon filament bulb provided a warm and slightly subdued light. Both of these latter two lamps were initially only manufactured by Louis Poulsen for the hotel, but became available in general retail several years later. Finally, a small wall lamp was designed with a spotlight-like effect and a similar appearance. It was only used in the rooms, where it sat on an electrical track that ran right over the dressing table, for example.

The original version and installation of the *Munkegård Lamp* can still be seen at Munkegård school. This ceiling-mounted lamp was widely used throughout the school. It protrudes slightly from the ceiling itself, which was largely an aesthetic decision to create a distinctive detail in the school's architecture. But it also served a function to provide cooling for the hot incandescent lamps used at the time, as well as to let some light out onto the ceiling surface to soften an otherwise harsh contrast between light and shadow.

AJ Park Light. This outdoor light was designed for Rødovre Town Hall in 1955. It came in two heights – a low one that reached roughly 120 cm above the ground, and a taller version of about 3 metres. This lighting manufactured by Louis Poulsen consists of a slightly conical milky white acrylic fixed to a post and lamp housing in galvanised steel tubing, which could potentially also be painted grey. This lamp was also used in large numbers at the entrance and parking area at Toms Fabrikker in Ballerup, which Jacobsen designed around 1960.

As mentioned, in the 1950s, things really picked up for Jacobsen's design studio in terms of large construction projects, not least for the public realm. Different lighting designs were drafted for several of these projects. The first was the *Munkegård Lamp* from 1956 which, as the name suggests, was developed for the school in Gentofte, which was designed and built between 1948 and 1957. It was a circular recessed ceiling lamp that was used throughout the school premises. The visible part of the lamp was an opal white glass plate with a diameter of 52.5 cm. The shade was edged with a thin brass band and mounted so that there was a small gap between the lamp shade and the surface of the ceiling. This construction provided ventilation to the original incandescent bulbs and helped to throw a little light onto the ceiling, which softens the otherwise harsh contrast between the luminous glass pane and the ceiling surface. The *Munkegård Lamp* was then included in Louis Poulsen's lamp programme and has since been used in many buildings, in particular offices and public spaces.

Later, between 1952 and 1956, Rødovre Town Hall was built. For this building, Jacobsen and his employees designed a wall lamp in 1955 that came to be called *Eklipta*. Inside the town hall, this lamp supplemented the widespread use of the *Munkegård Lamp*, but was placed exclusively on the walls, primarily in the stairwell areas.

It was a mouth-blown opal white glass lamp mounted to housing that was not built into the wall, but mounted on the outside of the wall surface. The lamp glass itself was lenticular with a relatively sharp edge. *Eklipta* was produced in two sizes for the town hall, one with a diameter of 45 cm and a smaller one of 35 cm. Jacobsen himself preferred the larger one for installation in the building's stairwells. It was also used outdoors, on the facade of the town hall. It was nicknamed the "Sailor's Hat" and a few years later was redesigned into a fixed table lamp with a somewhat smaller shade in connection with the construction of St Catherine's College in Oxford, where it was used in the dining room. Here it had a diameter of 22 cm.

THE 60S

Design in the basement

After quickly saying good morning to his employees in the basement and to Hans Dissing, who is sitting in the foreman's enclosure, Arne Jacobsen heads upstairs to talk to his secretary. She sits in the small room just as you head down to the basement. This is the heart of the design studio and is where all incoming and outgoing correspondence is recorded. This is where salaries and fees are kept in check, and perhaps most importantly, it's where a close eye is kept on the stock of pencils and erasers. Because employees must ask permission to obtain these vital tools. There is a special aura about the eraser. Because if you need one, it means you've drawn something wrong and wasted your time. It's a detail that Jacobsen pays close attention to.

Jacobsen walks out of his front door and the few hundred metres along the tiled walkway to the widow's townhouse, which is located next to the railway. He has rented the upper floor for employees who do not have space in his own basement. The young architects hide under the window and keep watch. Action stations. A captured mouse is released inside a fine model of a library with a glass-clear atrium. Jacobsen comes up the stairs, panting, and assumes his usual expression as he looks at the models and drawings, his head tilted and one eyebrow raised. Not a word. That model does seem a bit strange. Jacobsen maintains his poker face and makes a few aesthetic remarks, while the others bite their lips to keep themselves from giggling. It's only when he comes back and talks to Jonna that he bursts out laughing.

There's an upbeat atmosphere in the design studio. Most employees come directly from architecture school and are young men in their late twenties. Naturally, they bring the gags they picked up at the academy. There's smacking of rulers and erasers being thrown around. Although the design studio has grown from three men on Ørnegårdsvej in the late 1940s into one of the largest in Denmark, an informal and straightforward tone still prevails, often with cleverly conceived practical jokes.

Jacobsen starts his car and drives towards the city. He drives into Kongens Nytorv. In the old buildings of the National Bank of Denmark, which will soon be replaced by his own proposal, a small group of four or five architects are diligently drawing the new National Bank. It's here that his associate partner, Otto Weitling, keeps track of the projects, including the German ones. Like everyone else, Weitling was hired at the design studio right after he graduated – almost ten years ago now. He's from Southern Jutland and is bilingual Danish and German. He is sharp and articulate. Jacobsen would not have had the large design studio had it not been for Otto Weitling and design studio manager Hans Dissing, who ensure that deadlines and budgets converge into a harmonious whole. Dissing has also been there for more than 10 years.

As the design studio grew, Jacobsen bought a large villa on Svanemøllevej in Hellerup, which is his next stop on the drive. It's here that the major projects for West Germany, the UK, and Kuwait are designed, as well as the competition entries for contests across Europe. For Hannover, a flamboyant viewing pavilion resembling a leaf is planned. A leaf that Jacobsen picked up in the garden: "Can't you draw it like this?" he said, and had put the leaf on the table. Plans are also being drawn for a high school and a large headquarters in Hamburg, and work is underway on town halls elsewhere in Germany. These projects far exceed Aarhus, Søllerød, and Rødovre in scale. In the UK, plans are underway for a large hotel complex in Newcastle, a synagogue in Oxford, and a new Danish embassy in London.

It's a busy place, and many different languages are spoken. English and German are interspersed with French and Japanese.

Two young architects work late in the basement of the design studio under the townhouse on Strandvejen. It's clear how little space there is between the tables. The boss's office was a kind of foreman's enclosure, which can be seen in the background.

When Jacobsen turned 60, he was met with a torchlight procession by architecture students and colleagues in the courtyard of Charlottenborg. It was 1962, and he was a household name. His townhouse was filled with gifts, flowers, and congratulations. A few years earlier, he had built the Royal Hotel, where he had taken a quantum leap away from Danish coziness and restrained architecture. It was a jewel of international architecture and also Denmark's only skyscraper at the time. His design studio was now overflowing with large and prestigious commissions. St Catherine's College in Oxford was soon to be completed and marked Jacobsen's international format along with the major German projects.

↑ Jacobsen's 60th birth-
day was celebrated with
a torchlit procession
at Charlottenborg by

admiring students and
colleagues.

→ → Arne Jacobsen and
Otto Weitling admire
the model of one of their
many projects in West

Germany. It is one of their
most sculptural buildings.
The observation tower of
Herrenhausen Garten in

Frankfurt. It was supposed
to be where the main
building of the castle,
which was bombed during

the war, was located.
Unfortunately, only a small
foyer building was built.

Although Jacobsen had an economic and artistic impact that was far greater than that of his colleagues, this could not be seen in his surroundings. He lived in his modest townhouse, whose basement brimmed with young architects each morning. The reception rooms were used as a secretary's office and meeting room, so he and his wife's only real space was a bedroom and a living room. Then there was the garden, which at 400 square metre was smaller than the basement of the Klampenborg villas in the neighbourhood. His colleagues, such as Kay Fisker and Palle Suenson, behaved differently. Suenson even had a country house and the Queen's old Rolls-Royce. Jacobsen settled for a Citroën DS, although it couldn't fit in the garage, which was being used as a model workshop.

Jacobsen was a modest man, neither intellectual nor articulate. Unlike Alvar Aalto or Mies van der Rohe, he lacked a clear programme or a formulated ideology surrounding his architecture. He also didn't sit at his desk and draw that much himself, at least not during the infancy of a project. Instead he made suggestions based on his reading of trade journals, which he showed to his employees. It was then up to them to come up with their suggestions. In this way, the project was shaped in an interaction whereby Jacobsen directed and the young architects drew. When Knud Holscher had just started at the design studio and wanted to impress, he drew some proposals in the style of Jacobsen, but he got a scolding: "Draw it as you want it, and then I'll come in and get it how I want it later."

Ellen Waade shares this experience: "Although we worked quite freely, gradually we could see the project becoming a Jacobsen project." Imperceptibly, Jacobsen managed to turn things in his direction, while incorporating the employee's originality and massaging the cutting-edge modernity of international magazines into the project. "Now I want to decide on something," Jacobsen might exclaim when he joined meetings at the large design studio on Svanemøllevej. As the design studio grew, so did the distance from Jacobsen, and he became less involved in everything. It was a job he entrusted to his two faithful employees, Otto Weitling and Hans Dissing.

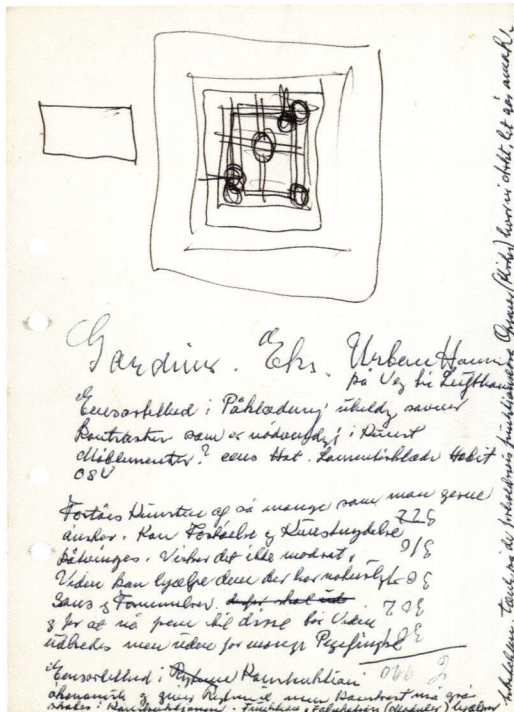

He could also be absent-minded and wasn't always aware of what he was doing, such as when he was faced with some drawings for the National Bank of Denmark and told Otto Weitling that he didn't like a particular elevation, to which Weitling replied that it was the floorplan and not an elevation he was looking at. Other design studios were quite well-organised and structured with neat drawings and details. With Jacobsen it was different, where the drawings could be lying in random rolls in a storage room and not always easy to find.

In a way, the design studio had not grown into a professional organisation. It was still Jacobsen's private playground, running with a certain degree of understaffing, and where time could be spent on the nitty-gritty. One thing Jacobsen spent a lot of time on was observing. Simply looking at the drawings and the models. When *Cylinda Line* was finished and ready to be photographed, Jacobsen spent ages finding the right angles to photograph the subjects from. Where did he get that time from? By delegating. His role was to choose and appoint.

When we listen to interviews with Jacobsen, we get a sense of his modesty and slightly clumsy language in a flat Copenhagen dialect. He was conscious of his own marketing in images and through the visual strength of his projects, but when it came to statements for newspapers and television, or at lectures, he could spend days pondering questions and answers. His clumsiness and not entirely well-considered statements could put him in the headlines, such as when he spoke critically about people's use of curtains in his buildings, knowing full well that he himself was dependent on the textile industry, as he had designed the most curtain patterns in Denmark. He was often mentioned in the newspapers and had to defend himself to the public, such as in the case of the Royal Hotel, which was popularly called the punch card (an early method of storing data) and was voted Denmark's ugliest building in a newspaper poll.

Jacobsen's design studio was a career-making catapult into the world of architecture. Many young architects worked for Jacobsen for a few years before moving on to other positions.

A key reason for the large turnover of employees at the design studio was the low salary. Jacobsen himself complained that the salaries were too high, because with international architects like Le Corbusier, young architects worked for free just to get the star's name on their CV.

Another reason for the influx of employees was the construction boom. Where Jacobsen had painstakingly built up his design studio by designing a plethora of single-family houses, things were different now. The young architects now set about designing universities and town halls.

Knud Holscher won the competition for Odense University together with Svend Axelsson. At the start of the 1930s, the two young men went from designing and supervising St Catherine's College and the National Bank of Denmark at Jacobsen's studio to building a university campus themselves. And Knud Munk won the competition for Roskilde County Hall.

However, you could clearly see that they had gone to a good school. The detailing and execution were a direct continuation of Jacobsen's eye for quality. But the style was their own and new.

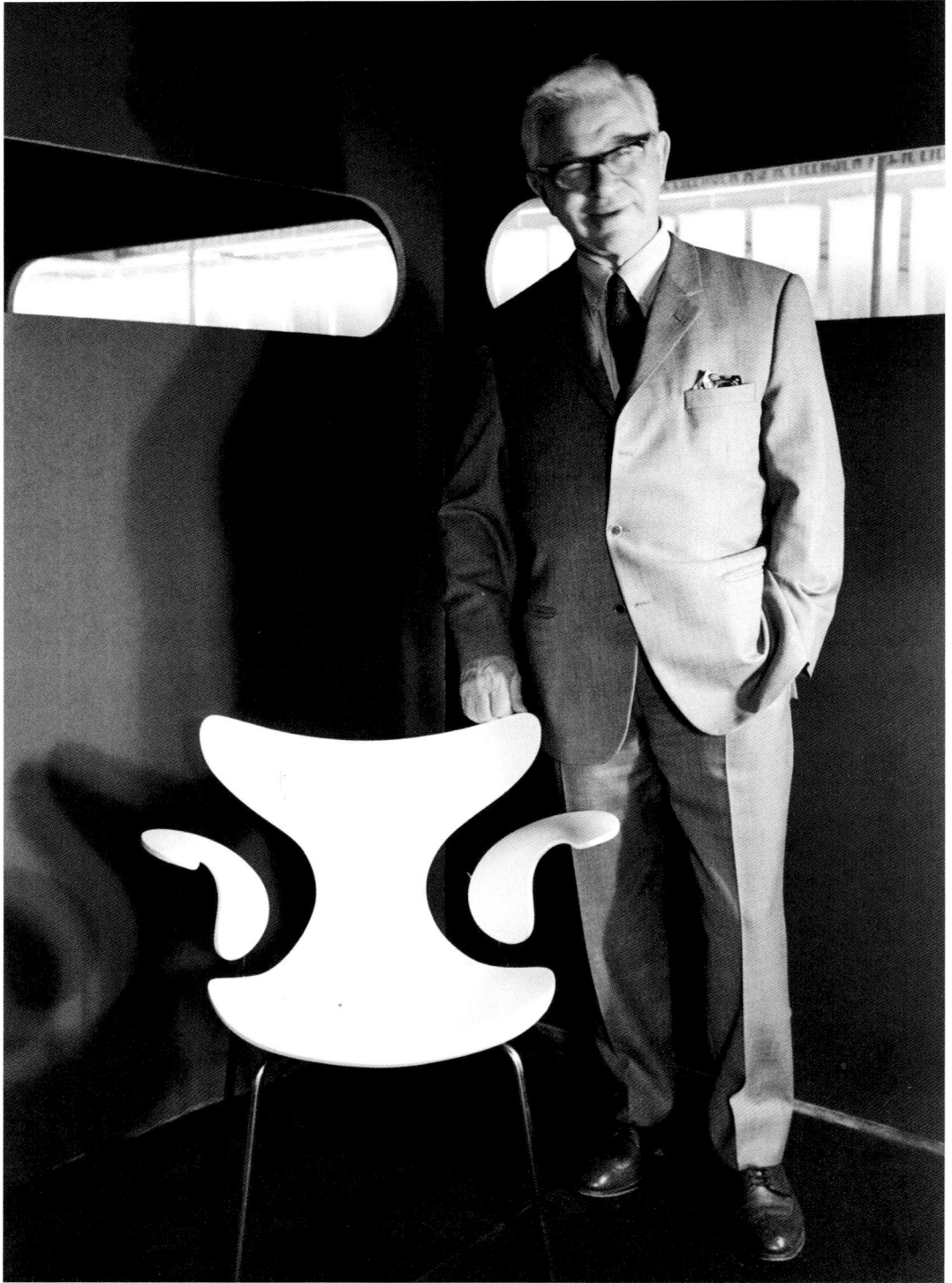

In the late 1950s and well into the prosperous years of the 1960s, Jacobsen found new ways to approach his work with design.

He became more searching and diverse in his design expressions, and there was not quite the same consistency in his aesthetics as before. Unlike before, in the 1960s he took on several external commissions, unrelated to the design studio's various building projects or his own ideas for new designs. Partnerships with a few permanent production companies such as Fritz Hansen and Louis Poulsen continued, but were now supplemented by other, also foreign,

companies. Some were direct continuations of previous successes, including new versions of the well-known shell chairs.

Throughout the 1960s and especially at the end of the decade, Jacobsen often returned to the shell chair, where it is the contour rather than the volume that describes the shape. In 1961, he designed a shell chair that was based on a seat shell from a *Series 7* chair, but which was milled into a slightly different shape. It was given the production name 3109 and could be interpreted as a more curved and rounded version of the *Series 7* which could

also be stacked. The construction principle was the same – nine layers of veneer moulded into a seat shell and mounted on four thin legs. The 3109 was briefly produced by Fritz Hansen, but was redesigned later in the decade and launched in 1968 as the 3108. Among other places, it was used in Rødovre Town Hall and, like the *Series 7*, could be equipped with horizontal coupling brackets so that it could be set up in rows for auditorium use. It was also produced in a children's edition, which was used in Rødovre Library, and a number of other places.

←Jacobsen with the last shell chair, the *Lily*, which he created for the many offices and canteen of the National Bank of Denmark. The shell is even more curved and three-dimensionally shaped than the previous shell chairs.

The edges are sanded, so the contour line is even sharper. Here he demonstrates his superior sense of aesthetics – the armrests seem to float freely in the air and perfectly emphasise the chair's waist shape.

The following year, in 1969, the 3108 was equipped with armrests that elegantly filled the waist of the chair's seat shell. It is the most aesthetically refined of the many shell chairs that came from Jacobsen's design studio over the years. The attached arms resemble wings, and the relationship between the curved shapes and the air between them gives the chair a superiorly beautiful shape. The version with armrests was given the product name 3208 and initially nicknamed the *Seagull*. The chair was used in the new building for the National Bank of Denmark alongside the 3108 in both pure wooden versions, with a veneer surface,

and in a lightly upholstered version. It was also introduced as an office chair in the National Bank of Denmark with a swivel base and wheels.

What the different models had in common, however, was that they were difficult to produce due to the significant curvatures of the seat shell, which meant that, at times, around 70% of production had to be discarded at Fritz Hansen's factory in Allerød, north of Copenhagen. Later, production of both the 3108 and 3208 was resumed using improved technology, and the chair was branded under the name *Lily*.

A fairly well-preserved prototype of the *Lily*. It was initially intended as a plastic chair. In the late 1960s, Arne Jacobsen and Fritz Hansen experimented extensively with plastic. But it was

too much for the factory. Note the different curve of the hind legs. It was an experiment that was abandoned in favour of the same design as the other stackable shell chairs.

It was the final attempt to extend the series of shell chairs from Jacobsen's design studio, simplifying and minimising the materials, while pushing the technology to its limits. Being able to insert just a single piece of bent pipe into the slot on the wooden back piece was a huge challenge – too huge, in fact. The chair was part of a broader experiment with different versions of office chairs.

→ Students at St Catherine's College reading newspapers and smoking in a true Jacobsen environment. The chairs are from the 3300 series, which was designed for Rødovre Town Hall.

Above the low tables, which were also designed by Jacobsen, hangs the *AJ Pendant*, which dates from 1957 and was designed in connection with the SAS hotel.

When Arne Jacobsen and Fritz Hansen looked to overseas in those years, they could see that new shapes and materials were on the way. Plastic, in particular, was now being used in furniture production. In terms of larger items, it was initially fiberglass that was used, such as in the shell chairs designed by Charles and Ray Eames, which are still in production today. Verner Panton's famous *Panton* chair was also initially produced in fiberglass, before it became possible to have it injection-moulded into a single piece of plastic a few years later. Meanwhile, Denmark's leading position in the field was up against fierce competition, with Italy taking over as the leading design country in Europe. Jacobsen's design studio therefore sketched out several new chairs in a different design language.

One of the new chairs was a small, lightweight affair with a separate seat and back. However, it never went into production, but could well have been produced in laminated wood had the technical issues been solved. Theoretically it could also have been made with a plastic seat and back, but it didn't get beyond the model stage. The chair was an extension of the long series of shell chairs but this time, as mentioned, it was in two parts. The seat was quite uncomplicated, almost completely flat, but the flimsy backrest created problems. It was intended to be held up only by a piece of bent pipe, mounted right in the line of symmetry, and the joint would be a vulnerable point in the construction due to the heavy loads that the twisting of the backrest would create. Incidentally, it is worth noting the somewhat different and rounder bend of the two hind legs on this prototype.

Another unrealised project was an office chair related to the shell chairs and intended for Fritz Hansen's product range. It was based on some kind of plastic, probably injection-moulded plastic. It was a highly sculptural chair that must have taken many hours to develop. We can follow the sketching process in a series of sketches by Jacobsen and his employees. But this chair also didn't get beyond a plaster mock-up as Fritz Hansen had neither the technology, the capital, nor the desire to start experimenting with producing furniture in these new and exotic materials. Other furniture architects such as Kay Kørbing and Leif Alring were making plastic furniture for Cadovius during the same period, and Verner Panton took the ultimate step by moving abroad to pursue the dream of plastic furniture.

A small series of relatively traditional furniture was designed for the rooms at St Catherine's College, named *Catherine*, and produced by Fritz Hansen.

There was a recliner, below, as well as a desk chair called *Etude*, like the one at the bottom of the opposite page.

In addition, a footstool was made to complement the armchair with a loose cushion that could be removed, enabling it to function as a small side table.

The armchair, which remained in production, came in both this slightly overworked version with milled shadow grooves and, later on, in a slightly simpler version. The chair was traditionally built with a springy seat and back and upholstery that popped up like a pillow, all to maintain the thin silhouette.

Some of the furniture that Fritz Hansen *was* ready to produce, however, were those that Jacobsen and his employees developed for the first of the major building projects that the firm designed following the Royal Hotel. These were mainly chairs, but also some tables for St Catherine's College in Oxford. This partially independent university with its own dormitory under the larger Oxford umbrella was designed and built around 1960 and inaugurated in 1964. Like the SAS hotel, St Catherine's was to become a gesamtkunstwerk, where Jacobsen created the building, landscaping, furniture, and other fixtures. To this end, two furniture series were designed, both of which

were presented at the inauguration and subsequently went into series production at Fritz Hansen, who was still Jacobsen's only partner in terms of furniture at that time.

The first furniture series was designed for the students' rooms and consisted of an armchair named *Catherine*, named after the college, of course. A desk with an accompanying chair and a footstool that could also be used as a stool or even as a low table if you removed the cushion. An internal competition at Fritz Hansen gave the chair the poetic name *Etude*. Design-wise, this furniture series looks relatively conventional, at least for a Jacobsen design.

There were no major technical challenges and no expressive forms, instead these were simple pieces in laminated light oak veneer put together to create functional furniture. The individual components of this furniture were visibly separated from each other, so you could see how they were put together. This was particularly pronounced in the armchair, where the pieces were mounted with visible black-chrome screw heads in the side rails. The armchair was also lightly upholstered, whereas the desk chair had no upholstery or cushion. It was neat and tidy, well-proportioned, but without the great surprising schwung that Jacobsen was otherwise known for.

← Arne and Jonna
Jacobsen with Alan
Bullock, who was the
driving force behind the
new building project
and called on Jacobsen
as the architect when he
was touring Danish and
foreign architects to find
the right expression for his
future dormitory.

→ The *Oxford* chair in the
veneered and low-backed
version with armrests and
the original wooden base
(see also pages 253 and
261). This photo probably
shows more of a refined
prototype than an actual
production model.

The second furniture design for St Catherine's College was somewhat more stylish. It was later named the *Oxford* chair when the series was introduced to the wider market in 1965. It started as just a single, very high-backed chair, specifically intended for the professor's table in the dining room. It has a very formal appearance, almost with a Shaker-like asceticism. When the teachers sat on it at their separate dinner table in the great hall, it seemed as if they were in their own closed room, because the only thing you could see from a distance was the high backs of the chairs. Such scenography reflects the ancient British university tradition of ranking according to age and status, simply updated with modern Danish design.

The Royal Hotel and St Catherine's College are two of Jacobsen's great holistic designs. Where the SAS hotel's interior is driven by innovation, plastic, and organic shapes, St. Catherine's is tempered by older virtues with wood as one of the focal points. For the Royal Hotel, Jacobsen designed the interiors – including the furniture, lamps, and door handles – in soft and organic forms to evoke a humanising effect in relation to the strict look of the building itself in glass and steel. For the prestigious college, however, in one of the world's oldest universities with classical and perhaps somewhat rigid traditions, Jacobsen's design studio created a rather sober and tightly composed building with exposed concrete structures and raw brick walls in an almost brutalist design language. Here, the furniture came to play into and perhaps even emphasise the almost puritanical college.

At the inauguration, the entire dining hall in St Catherine's resembled a hypermodern version of Hogwarts from the Harry Potter universe. The students sat at long tables on equally long backless benches under the bare, slender concrete beams that held up the ceiling.

The light came either from above the high windows or from the low-placed table lamps, which Jacobsen had also designed. It was the so-called *Eklipta* lamp that was nicknamed the *Sailor's Hat*. Although St Catherine's College was a highly successful piece of architecture, the design was less commercially successful.

The *Oxford* chair's seat shell was made from a long and wide piece of laminated veneer. It was very thin, and from the side it could be perceived almost as one long line drawn freehand with a soft, thick pencil.

From the front, it appears almost square, cut completely straight at the top and sides and with only the necessary rounded corners.

In the original version, the shell was placed on a base consisting of four laminated wooden profiles, mounted in a cross shape. It had no upholstery, remaining pure in form and expression, emphasising the asceticism of the entire college project. However, the construction with a wooden base proved to be too fragile and was quickly changed to a cruciform cast aluminium frame. A step backwards aesthetically, perhaps, but functionally necessary. A version of the *Oxford* chair with a low back was also developed, which was identical to its big brother in all other respects. The furniture for St Catherine's was produced by Fritz Hansen, who was also responsible for the product development of standard models for the broader market. A number of variants were manufactured and sold from the mid-1960s and have since been modified and adjusted in terms of the frame, armrests, upholstery, and colours. Some models also came with wheels so they could function as office chairs. Various versions are still being marketed at the time of writing.

For Fritz Hansen, the order for furniture for St Catherine's College was a good one.

It was the company's largest order to date, and it was far larger than the order for the Royal Hotel. Fritz Hansen's design studio manager at the time was Jørgen Viggo Hansen, who otherwise faced criticism for his way of winning the order. On Jacobsen's orders, he sent all the prototypes express by plane to London. Søren Hansen was furious and saw the money flowing out of the company, but the following week the order was approved by the board, and he had to apologise to his design studio manager.

Even though Jacobsen received far more in annual royalties than the two Hansen brothers earnt together, it was a good partnership. Every time Jacobsen completed a building, Fritz Hansen was called upon to furnish it. Jacobsen did not allow other people's furniture in his buildings. In the 1960s, the projects had grown in floor space and volume. Thanks to Jacobsen's publishing technique with beautiful pictures in foreign magazines and his own exhibitions, this was invaluable advertising for Fritz Hansen. Also because many other architects had their buildings filled with Jacobsen's furniture.

→ The original version of the *Oxford* chair with a laminated shell. Unlike the newer versions it is not upholstered, but exclusively veneered. In addition, there is the original wooden base. Seen from the front or from behind, as on the opposite page, the chair appears to be quite flat and straight in shape. Seen from the side as here, it's clear how the seat shell is modelled with the intention of fitting the user's body.

← The dining hall of St Catherine's College with its original furnishings. The professor's table is in the foreground and the students' long tables and benches in the background.

The references to centuries-old traditions are clear, now brought to life by Harry Potter's schooling at Hogwarts. You can also see the fixed table lamps, also designed by Jacobsen, which were nicknamed *Sailor's Hats*. The space is extremely soberly designed, both architecturally and in terms of the furnishings. It was a style that became known as brutalism, and where the raw concrete structures and untreated materials appeared bare and somewhat crude in expression.

This is one of Jacobsen's "large rooms". Although the space has been preserved, the furnishings have been changed, with the low benches replaced with *Series 7* chairs.

The sketching process at the design studio was often initiated by young employees free-hand sketching small models. Jacobsen didn't interfere here.

The tilting chair is definitely the most traditional chair designed by Jacobsen. But there was a gap in Fritz Hansen's product range that needed to be filled. He used the furniture in his holiday home, most likely because it was free. Otto Weitling believed that Jacobsen compromised when he built his holiday home. His normal aesthetic credo was "as thin as possible and never in the middle," which was a typical modernist norm. But for the holiday home, the slogan was changed to "preferably in the middle, if it's free."

The *Oxford* series was the last furniture series from the master's hand to be released to the wider market. It was as too many different directions were pursued at the design studio in the 1960s, and Jacobsen's brand lost ground. He had to look a little harder to find the design expressions that met the needs of the time, which he had been so good at identifying and exploiting in previous decades. Various attempts were made to develop new furniture, but they were not really successful.

In 1965, a series of chairs called *Tilt* with accompanying side tables was introduced. These were traditionally machine-crafted armchairs with upholstered seats and backs. Classic in light wood, these simple furniture collections were ready to be put into production anywhere. It was something completely different from what Jacobsen had been known for until now. If you didn't know it was a Jacobsen design, you never would have guessed it. The industry was equally shocked. They were reportedly designed for Jacobsen's own new holiday home, which was an old converted farmhouse north of Slagelse, close to the small lake Tissø. The series was briefly put into production at Fritz Hansen.

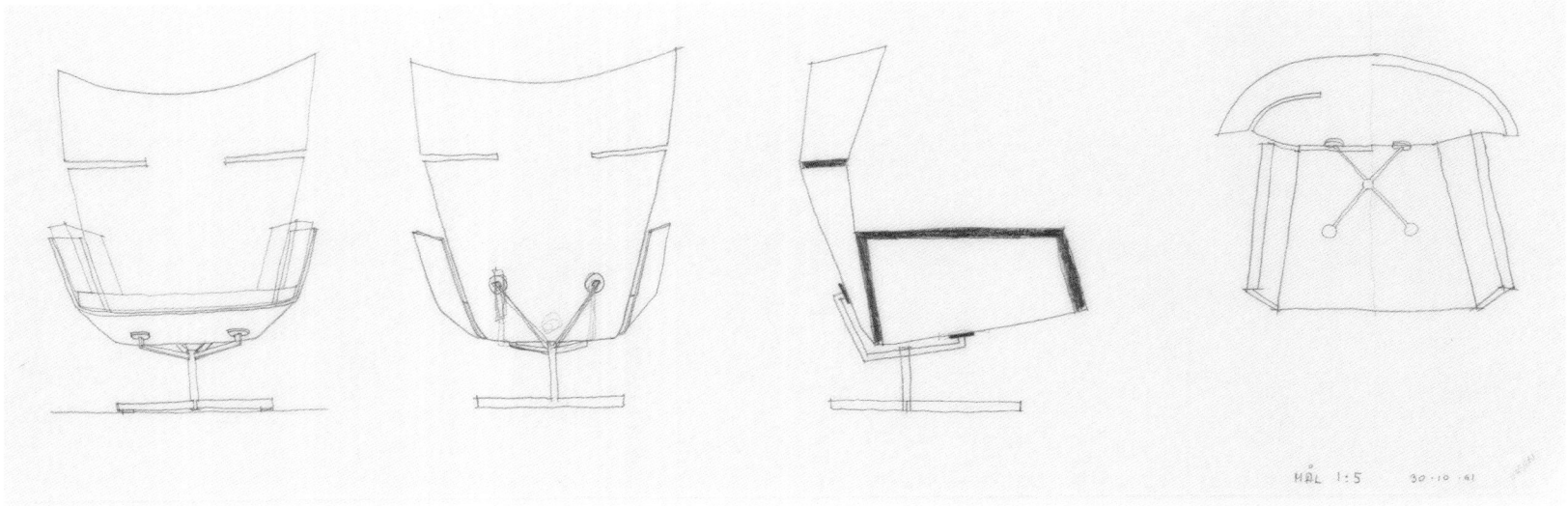

Another example is a kind of radical update of the *Egg*, which was called the *Ox*. Both of these large armchairs can be seen as a modern interpretation of the classic wingback chair. The *Ox* was designed in 1966 as a large, wide armchair on a swivel base, fully upholstered in leather and with a five-prong aluminium base. There is something almost samurai-like about this chair, and perhaps it was a little too big and different for private buyers at the time. In any case, it didn't last long on the market. However, many years later, Fritz Hansen put it back into production. Larger homes and different lifestyles perhaps made it more acceptable in living rooms. A smaller version of the chair with a fixed cross frame was developed, but never went into production.

A chair called the *Ox*. At the top are a series of sketches for a lighter lounge chair. A prototype is built and stands in Jacobsen's office on Svanemøllevej. The motif was developed further and applied to the large 'father's chair', which was then named the *Ox*.

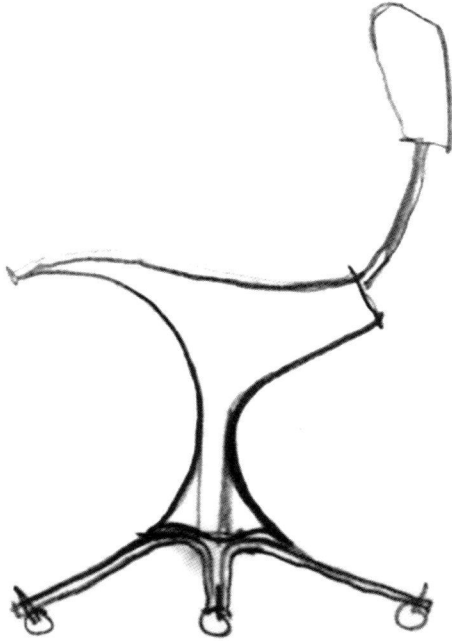

→→ A photo taken from above of a circle of chairs named *Snoopy*, the cartoon dog.

This low lounge furniture was designed for the city hall project in the German city of Mainz.

The chair came in both a straight and curved version, so it could be set up in a variety of shapes, such as in a circle as we see here, and in other cases as a row of chairs that snaked through a larger room. It was

approved by Jacobsen just before he died. In the early 1970s, Fritz Hansen really opens his eyes to modern tubular steel furniture and pursues the development of this new product with Verner Panton.

The futuristic office chair that never came to fruition. At the top is an early, simple sketch, and at the bottom are two pictures of the plaster

model that Jacobsen and his employees modelled in full size. The final material would be some kind of plastic, but it didn't progress,

probably because Fritz Hansen didn't want to start producing plastic chairs at that time with the prospect of uncertain financial returns.

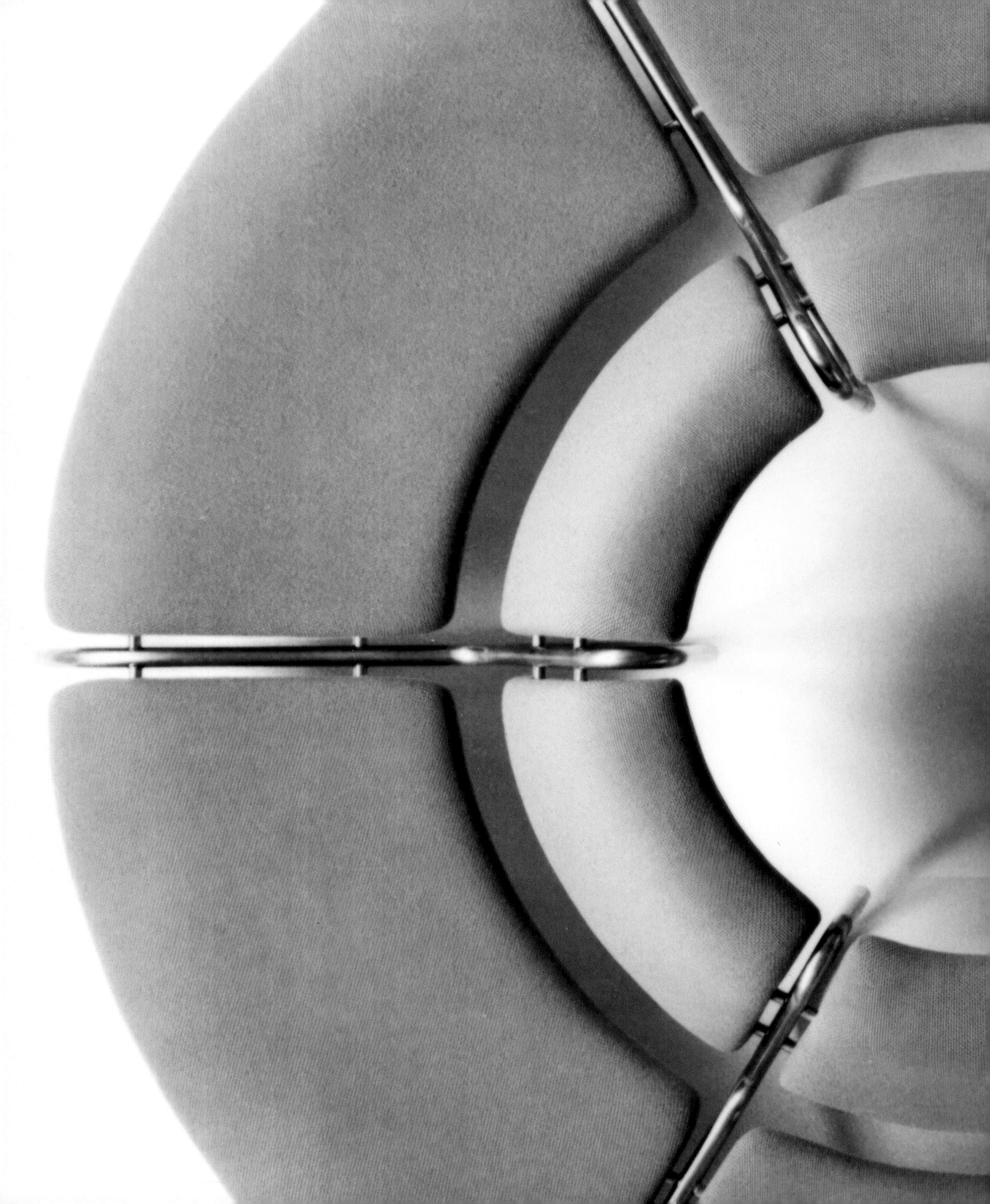

Another armchair series, called the *TV* chair, was designed in 1970. It was an armchair consisting of a somewhat complicated metal frame with rectangular upholstery elements and an accompanying footstool in the same style. Again, it was Fritz Hansen who manufactured it, and again only for a short period.

The last chairs that Jacobsen managed to draw and approve the prototype of before his death in 1971 were the 3600 series. They were initially designed for the city hall in the German city of Mainz, which the design firm was in the process of completing at the time. The series was nicknamed *Snoopy*

and consisted of various steel tube furniture with upholstered seats and backs, which were intended for waiting areas. The chairs were very low with a seat height of just 32 cm, and so correspondingly low tables were also developed. It was again Fritz Hansen who produced this furniture, which was marketed for a few years without any major commercial success. The sides consisted of chrome-plated steel tubes, designed as several interconnected circles. The chair was a modern snake style, meaning that several elements could be connected together to form a snake or circle that could wind through a large hall or lobby.

Fritz Hansen may have known that something was up with Jacobsen's newly developed furniture – they were no longer big sellers. Evident in the fact that they had started working on other, similar series with their next house designer. A few years later, Verner Panton made a similar furniture system in steel wire – the *Pantonova* series followed by his versatile *System 1-2-3* collection. There was even an *Oxford* chair with a high back – now in Panton's playful shapes.

New paths and new habits – Jacobsen in the so-called *TV* chair for Fritz Hansen. It's a little bit Eames, a little bit dentist. All the furniture that didn't relate to the shell chairs or the *Swan* or the *Egg* quickly went out of production again. They lacked that touch that Jacobsen was otherwise known for.

→ → Cardboard model of a chair for the Finnish furniture factory Asko. Here, Eero Aarnio was the chief designer and designed his version of the *Egg*, called *The Ball* *Chair*, which was even more radical and had just a slanted cut, straight down through a ball shape. It's as if Jacobsen wanted to break new ground and dabble in the world of plastic fantasy, but the chairs continued to be made of the sure and steadfast material, plywood.

↖ ↓ The series for Mainz City Hall consisted of a side piece, which was composed of a series of circular strokes and an equally low accompanying table. The idea of creating a furniture system that could be put together to make different shapes was a new, but fairly typical development within both furniture and architecture at this time. This can also be seen in the design studio's work with prefabricated and modular small houses.

Furniture for Asko

There had been a cultural revolution in the early 1960s, driven primarily by young people. The LP record and the hit single became a fixture in many children's and young people's bedrooms. This gave rise to a completely different self-understanding than the one still experienced from the state-authorised television in the living room.

Jacobsen, who always had his antennas out, was a particular fan of the Danish children's television programme Ingrid og Lillebror. It was an innocent series with a puppet and a kind teacher character. Whether he gained any deeper understanding of young people's sources of inspiration from this seems doubtful. But he was a curious type, leading him to question the young employees of the design studio about things like the effects of hashish. A year before his death, he visited his old employee Verner Panton at his exhibition Visiona 2 at the furniture fair in Cologne. The exhibition consisted of an environment of psychedelic floating furniture. Verner Panton and the German textile company Bayer had together created an amazing space age-like textile-covered fantasy landscape that you could sit, lie, and walk in, boasting Verner Panton's well-known colour palettes ranging from blue and orange to yellow and purple.

Verner Panton moved to Basel in the early 1960s to be close to his main client Vitra. It was here that, after a long development process, he created his moulded Panton chair. During these years, Panton released one hit after another onto the design scene, culminating in Visiona 2. He had now become one of the

↘ The two chairs that became something at Asko. Both are based on the same principle of interlocking sheets of plywood. The comfort was not overwhelming. The Prepop chair on the left and the Rover Chair on the right.

↓ Small model sketches for a chair in fiberglass and a more traditional version in steel tubes and plywood.

world's most recognised designers. Jacobsen had followed him throughout the years, and they considered each other good friends. Jacobsen could see that the winds were turning in furniture design. Furniture could now sit lower and be much more organic. It could even be in shiny, glossy, and colourful plastic, often in red and orange like Verner Panton's furniture. Even Braun's ascetic white-grey hair dryers and shavers changed colour to bright orange.

A significant exponent of this trend was the Finnish designer Eero Aarnio. In the early 1960s, he was employed as a design studio manager for the Finnish furniture company Asko and was now working as a designer for them. He designed as freely and imaginatively as Verner Panton when it came to plastic and colours, designing the *Ball*, *Pastil*, and *Bubble*, which were presented on the international stage between 1966 and 1968.

Ball and *Bubble* were a direct continuation of Jacobsen's *Egg*, but now as completely enveloping high-backed armchairs. It is therefore no wonder that it was Eero Aarnio who brought Jacobsen on board for a new furniture adventure.

Jacobsen designed several pieces of furniture for the Finnish furniture manufacturer Asko in the late 1960s, including a laminated chair called *Prepop*, which was produced in relatively few copies around 1970. It is reportedly a rather uncomfortable chair, which should probably be considered an experiment in shape typical of the time. It came in many colours, and parts of the same design could also function as a kind of table trestle. Jacobsen also designed the *Rover* armchair for Asko, which was a piece of quasi self-assembled furniture. It hit the spirit of the times very well by being slightly caricatured in its aesthetics. The individual parts of the chair are somewhat oversized, and even in this design it is difficult to see Jacobsen's usual expression.

The archives also contain full-size drawings and photos of small models of some other plastic chairs. They were photographed in the garden on Svanemøllevej and must date to sometime in the late 1960s. We don't know exactly, but we assume these are sketches for some upcoming Asko chairs. They are clearly inspired by none other than Verner Panton and Eero Aarnio.

Reaching out into the world

In the first years after the shell chairs were introduced, Jacobsen received flattering enquiries from foreign manufacturers who were eager to see similarly large collections designed for them. None led to a partnership, probably because Jacobsen was most pleased with his fruitful collaboration with Fritz Hansen. With the informal and workshop-like weekly meeting, full of prototypes and ideas, it would probably have been too much to initiate partnerships elsewhere, not least because of the distances and language barriers involved.

Looking at the estate inventory after Jacobsen's death in 1971, we can see several contracts with German, English, and Irish companies that have just been signed and that seem promising. So perhaps at this point he actually felt capable of staffing and managing a larger design studio. He certainly had an appetite for pursuing directions other than the one he took with Fritz Hansen. One company he carried out a project for was the Israeli manufacturer IDC. This can be seen from some surviving and fairly accurate drawings of a chair, a table, and a daybed. Here he mixes the ultra-comfortable with stylistic features from the Bauhaus era. It was also a project that stopped upon his death.

The office furniture series *djob* in an exhibition at the Danish Museum of Art and Design. Shown here is a desk along with a pair of side tables, one of which has space for hanging files and other forms of storage. Furthermore, *djob* is surrounded by nothing but Jacobsen's design: A *Series 7* office chair, two high-backed *Oxford* chairs and various *AJ Lamps*.

↑ The small *Eklipta* lamp, nicknamed the *Sailor's Hat*, fixed to the tables at St Catherine's College, Oxford.

↓ Jacobsen challenged technology, and this was especially evident with his last pendant lamp in opal glass, which he designed for St Catherine's College.

The mouth-blown shape was simply too difficult and the rejection rate was too high, so Louis Poulsen had to take it out of production.

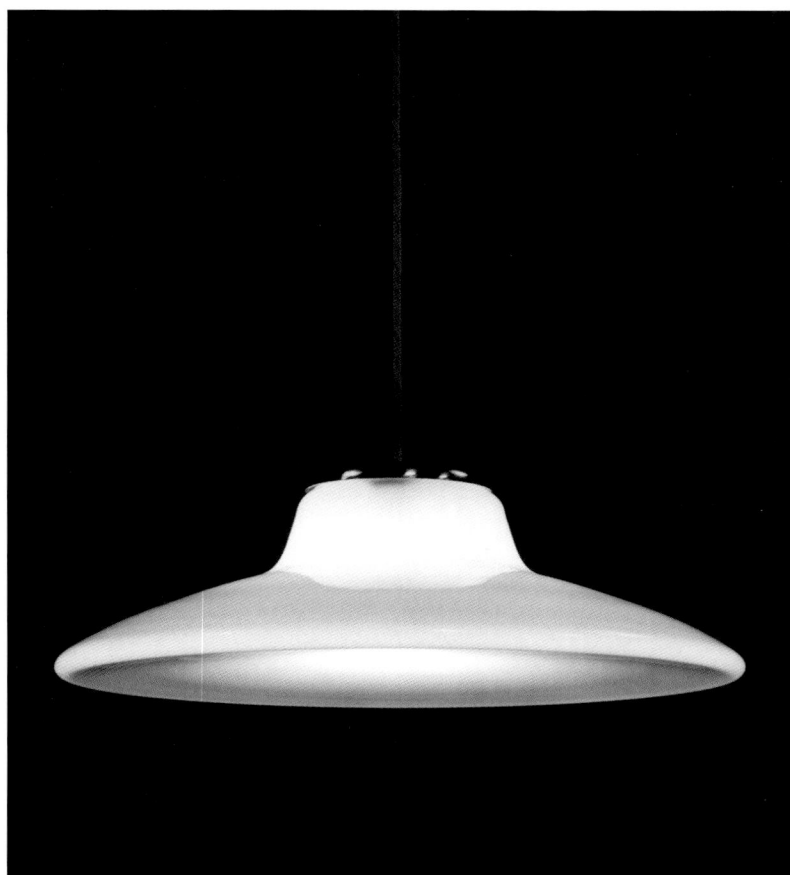

Throughout the years, Jacobsen had made special furnishings for town and city halls, schools and, not least, Novo. But in the 1960s, a structure and a final proposal for a complete system for the contract market were still lacking. Perhaps for no other reason than because the design studio was working on increasingly larger commissions throughout the 1960s, with representative buildings, which required different and more modern types of furniture. This was reflected in the Royal Hotel and partly also in St Catherine's College. Consequently, office furniture was designed directly for the commissions, such as for the large office building for Hamburg's electricity plant HEV (now Vattenfall). The hope was then to be able to collect them into a saleable collection. For a number of years, Munch Møbler had had the ambition to create a complete office furniture series, and many prototypes had also been made. But the process had been lengthy and died out after a while.

It was the newly started company djob that was given the task of producing Jacobsen's only mass-produced office furniture series, which was initially developed as a model and prototype for the National Bank of Denmark. This series was in the new, modern, slightly soft style, with rounded corners and downward sloping table edges that can make breadcrumbs disappear with a flick. The construction consists of flat aluminium tubes joined at the corners by plastic sleeves – not really very precise or elegant. The desks could be equipped with side tables with swivel heads for the new IBM typewriters, hanging filing cabinets and other drawer arrangements, as well as planters. One might say that this was Arne Jacobsen in a nutshell.

One of the major projects that Jacobsen undertook, and which did not arise directly from a construction project, was the tabletop series *Cylinda Line* for the company Stelton. It was launched in 1967, but had been several years in the making due to the technical challenges involved in working with the pure cylindrical shapes in stainless steel. The design process began when Jonna Jacobsen's son from her first marriage, Peter Holmblad, was employed by the company Stelton in 1963. He thought they lacked a modern and high-quality design line in stainless steel.

Once a week, Peter came for dinner and started working on his stepfather to get him to draw some modern designs for Stelton. After some time, he wore Jacobsen down. And once Jacobsen agreed to a project, he was committed and accorded it all his passion and stubbornness with regard to the finish and details that he was so well-known for. So Peter got his frame, which was named *Cylinda Line*, and received an ID award for it that same year. However, it didn't sell very well, so he bought most of the pieces back. In this way, the stores could see that there was money to be made, which helped.

Originally, the idea was to use a piece of stainless steel dairy piping and weld the base on, but this required too much machining to achieve the right finish. So instead, the items ended up being pressed and rolled from a sheet of the hard and difficult metal. The long wait for the launch was due to Peter Holmblad and Stelton wanting to launch a larger product line all at once instead of gradually introducing new items to the series. There were 18 separate pieces in the *Cylinda Line* series by the time it was unveiled in 1967. The series was photographically depicted as a Manhattan-style skyline in meticulously matte brushed stainless steel.

During these years, Jacobsen worked along various aesthetic lines, one of which was the distinctive cylindrical motif. As always,

Jacobsen was very concerned with how his architecture and design were photographed and displayed in catalogues, magazines, and at exhibitions. The *Cylinda Line*, which he designed for the company Stelton, is depicted here as a Manhattan skyline and shows the first 18 products launched in 1967, which include various jugs, ashtrays, cocktail shakers, ice buckets, and more.

he placed great emphasis on ensuring that everything was in order in terms of design and that the quality and finish were top notch. He gave thorough consideration to the processing and composition of the materials. For example, the metal parts should have a perfect shine, and no other traces of processing should be visible other than the perfect matte brushed quality of the stainless steel. Similarly, the matte black plastic handles should have fairly sharp edges, regardless of the fact that this could making carrying a full jug fairly uncomfortable.

Just as many of Jacobsen's furniture designs had a clear and distinct separation between the individual components, as can be seen in his shell chairs, there was also a distance between the body and the handle in *Cylinda Line*. This was for both aesthetic and practical reasons. This made adapting the production of the various components easier, and also prevented gaps between the two parts, which could collect dirt.

More parts for the large set were added in the following years. *Cylinda Line* included everything, from ice buckets and cream jugs to ashtrays and pepper shakers. The only product Jacobsen didn't manage to design for the series was a thermos. A young ceramicist named Erik Magnussen would take over the task. He went on to become the next preferred designer for Stelton.

The aforementioned barrel-shaped *Prepop* chair, designed for Finnish Asko, was part of this cylindrical style, which was among Jacobsen's favourite design markers in the 1960s. For the last of his major domestic building projects, the National Bank of Denmark in Copenhagen, this shape was also used for a series of fixtures known as *Vola*. It was the manufacturer Verner Overgaard who owned the factory I.P. Lund, who contacted Jacobsen and asked for help designing a built-in tap that the company had developed. The idea was that most of the technology could be hidden inside the masonry, and only the tap itself and the handle

would be visible and protrude from the wall. It was a simplicity that Jacobsen appreciated, so he designed the simplest possible handle and spout, again using cylindrical shapes. The components were originally supposed to have a satin chrome finish, but this was not possible, and so the idea arose to launch *Vola* in brightly coloured finishes, something that was quite new at the time.

The architect Teit Weylandt worked on the project and subsequently also designed the many accessories that formed a large and commercially important part of the system. This included soap dispensers, hooks, mirror brackets, toothbrush holders, shelf supports, and the like. This resulted in a large product family, but also a system of combinable modules that could be compiled according to what best suited the bathroom. There was also a large variation in the size of the taps, for example. Some were short, others long or swivelling, while others worked as shower heads or had other features.

In 1969, Jacobsen entered into an agreement with the British sanitary ware manufacturer Ideal Standard to develop a toilet series. By the time of his death, the project had been outlined with detailed, full-scale drawings. Peter Denney, who was the firm's representative in Newcastle, took care of contact. It was perhaps not the most practical sanitary ware series that saw the light of day here. The idea seems to be that since Jacobsen was entering the market for prefabricated houses, it would be appropriate for him to have a complete set of sanitary ware for these projects. That would be *Vola* with taps and shower heads alongside Ideal Standard's sanitary ware.

Both series should have been introduced and included in the interiors of the National Bank of Denmark.

In addition to *Vola*, which was something of a tap trendsetter with its cylindrical shapes that sat perpendicular to each other and round bar handle, there were several subsequent products with the same design expression. To this end, the series for Ideal Standard was also a precursor to the idea that the toilet bowl and washbasin could be a sculptural element in the bathroom. The project was unfortunately abandoned when the managing director of the British company left and Jacobsen died.

Vola was completely different from other taps when it came on the market. These often had curved shapes that reflected the flow of the water. But Jacobsen defied the laws of nature and forced the water to flow through a bent cylindrical tube. If emulation is anything to go by, *Vola* was a success, with many taps copying its design.

Jacobsen continued with plumbing fixtures. He developed a sanitary ware series for the British company Ideal Standard, with a toilet, bidet, and washbasin in the same design language. The motif was a sliced egg shape set on a sharply cut plinth. The project was well underway and many technical drawings were complete when the company ended the project following Jacobsen's death.

The design studio would most certainly have had all the design and architecture magazines of the time on display. These served as a well of inspiration that Jacobsen tapped into to create his next piece. He poured over the magazines on a daily basis. One particular magazine in the stack that caught his eye was Peter Cook and the British group Archigram's brightly coloured and very cartoonish defence of the changing city and housing. In precise technical drawings combined with Marvel's comic book style, proposals were shown for so-called Plug-In Cities and Walking Cities – a system for how the city – like in the old science fiction comics where humans lived on Mars – could connect to and enrich other cities such as New York and London.

On a different scale, they had proposals for how, with minimal construction, one could create an inflatable dwelling that could grow out of a body-hugging spacesuit. The funny thing about this project was that when two individuals fell in love and wanted to sleep with each other, a cartoon sequence depicted how their spacesuits also "morphed" together.

Although the ideas of these magazines have not been directly translatable into usable architecture, they certainly inspired everyone in that generation of architects. However, there were a number of people, especially British architects such as Richard Rogers and Norman Foster, who used this constructive style rather directly. Perhaps most clearly in the giant cultural centre that Renzo Piano and Richard Rogers built in Paris, known as the Centre Pompidou. Here, everything was turned inside out and installations were visibly led over the roof and out the back of the building as large decorative elements. This was a motif that Arne Jacobsen's design studio gradually used in the unrealised Roskilde University Centre, where technical installations serve as exposed ornaments for the first time in Danish architecture.

↓ Illustrations of the *Kubeflex* system, the modular building concept, where standard cubes could be put together to form larger or smaller buildings, such as a holiday home or even a primary home, as well as kindergartens and the like. At the top left, we can see the finished solution drawn with cross-sections of four of these cubes, while the illustration beneath shows a facade drawing with shading. On the right is a series of floor plans showing how the system has almost infinite combinations.

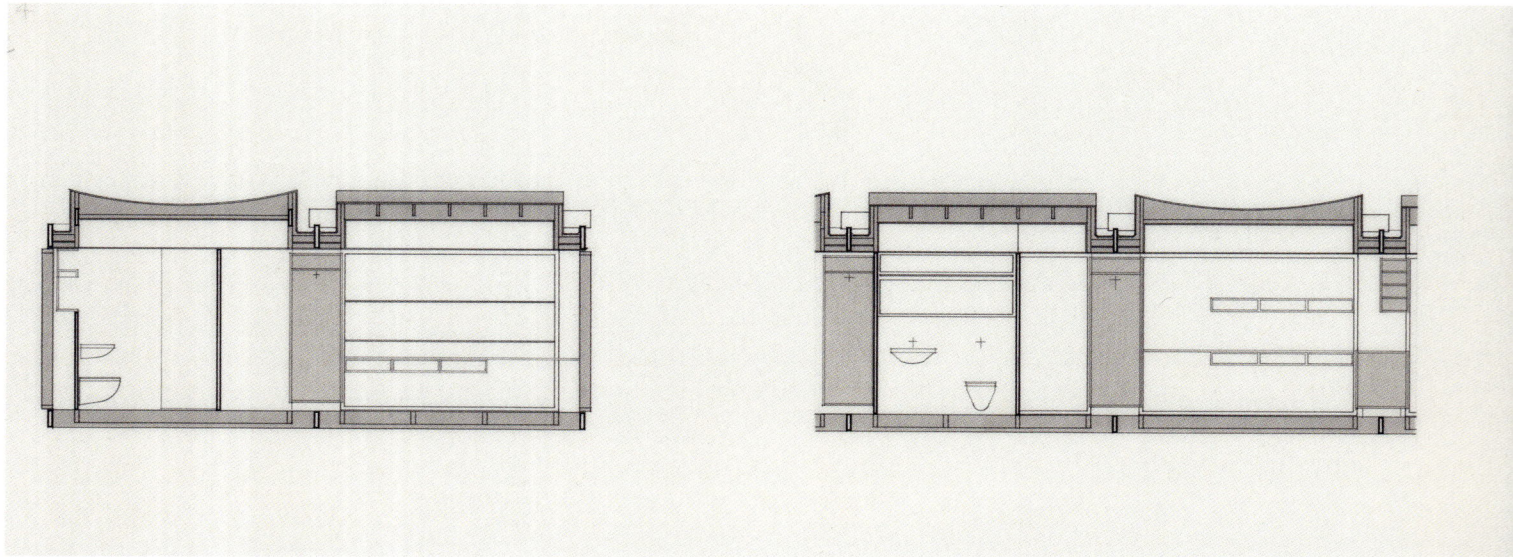

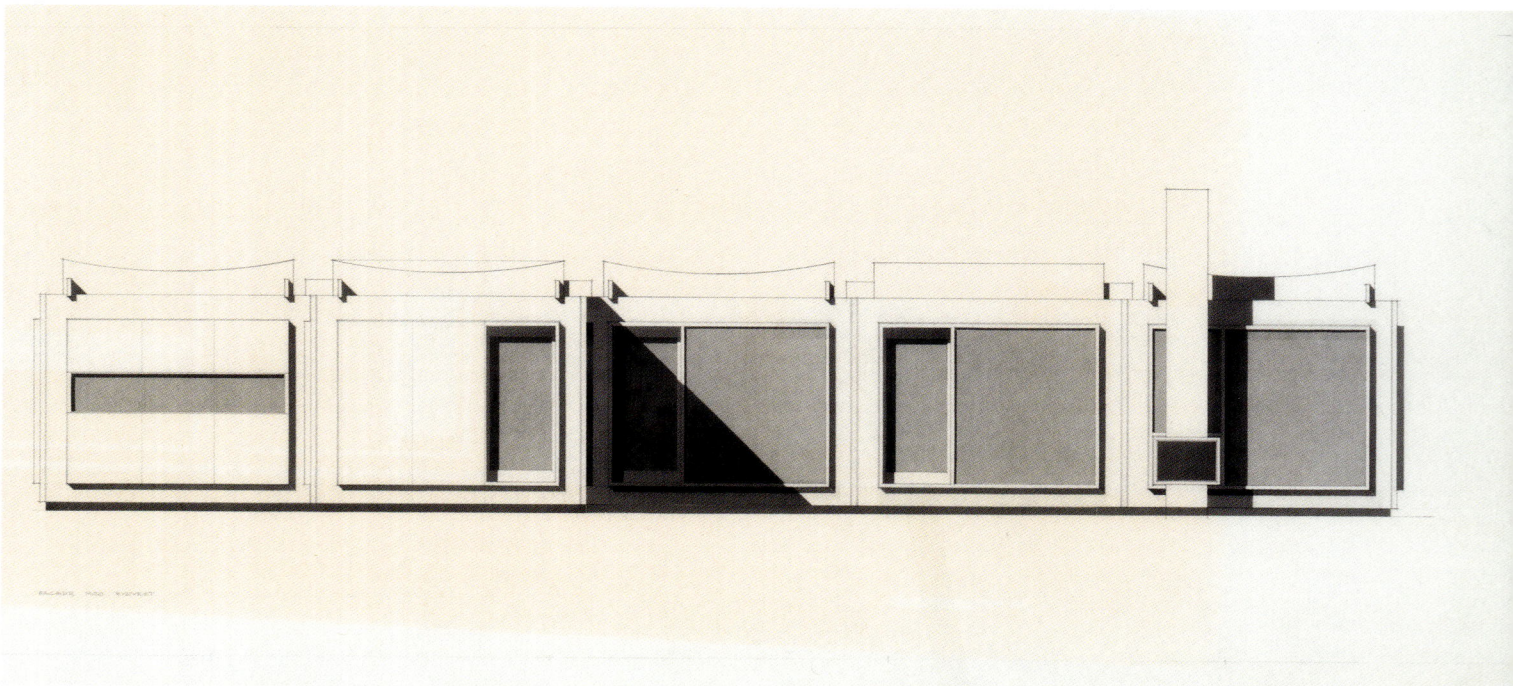

In the year before his death, Jacobsen worked on several stock house projects. It was an unusual concept called the *Mill House*, which had a fan-shaped floor plan, but this never made it further than the drawing board. It was a more ordinary stock house created from concrete elements, which we know so well today. Two other concepts for stock houses were approached differently. These were wooden structures made of glulam timber, which were placed on a light foundation. They were given the distinctive names *Kubeflex* and *Kvadraflex*. As their names suggest, these were square floor plans with flexible modules that allowed everything from small family houses to kindergartens and even larger buildings to be built using the same elements. They were to be built around a core for the utilities, and the heat was to be provided by electric panels installed in the transition to the ceiling tiles.

The idea was to build homes that could be adapted to the needs of the individual family through the different phases of life and family. It was a timely approach. Jørn Utzon touched on the same issue with his *Expansiva* building system, which alluded to the possibility of expansion. A contemporary parallel to this dream are the not particularly pretty, but still functional shed or container cities that can be set up quickly and connected together with a crane at construction sites or used for refugee camps, student housing, temporary school classrooms, or even makeshift hospital wards.

The aim with *Kubeflex* and *Kvadraflex* was to provide an holistic design for the space, supplemented with the sanitary ware from *Vola* and Ideal Standard, and with an interior that formed a cohesive whole. It would be the elaborate Jacobsen-esque gesamtkunstwerk, where everything was co-ordinated, a free-flowing space, and a home that could be scaled up or down in size as needed. When the family grew, they simply added a children's room. But removing it again once they had flown the nest was a concept lost in the mists of the future. However, the projects were still too demanding – the test houses were completed a few months after Jacobsen's death and were later moved several times. They were initially used as the son's holiday home and later moved to the Trapholt Museum for Modern Art and Design in Kolding as a permanent outdoor exhibition pavilion.

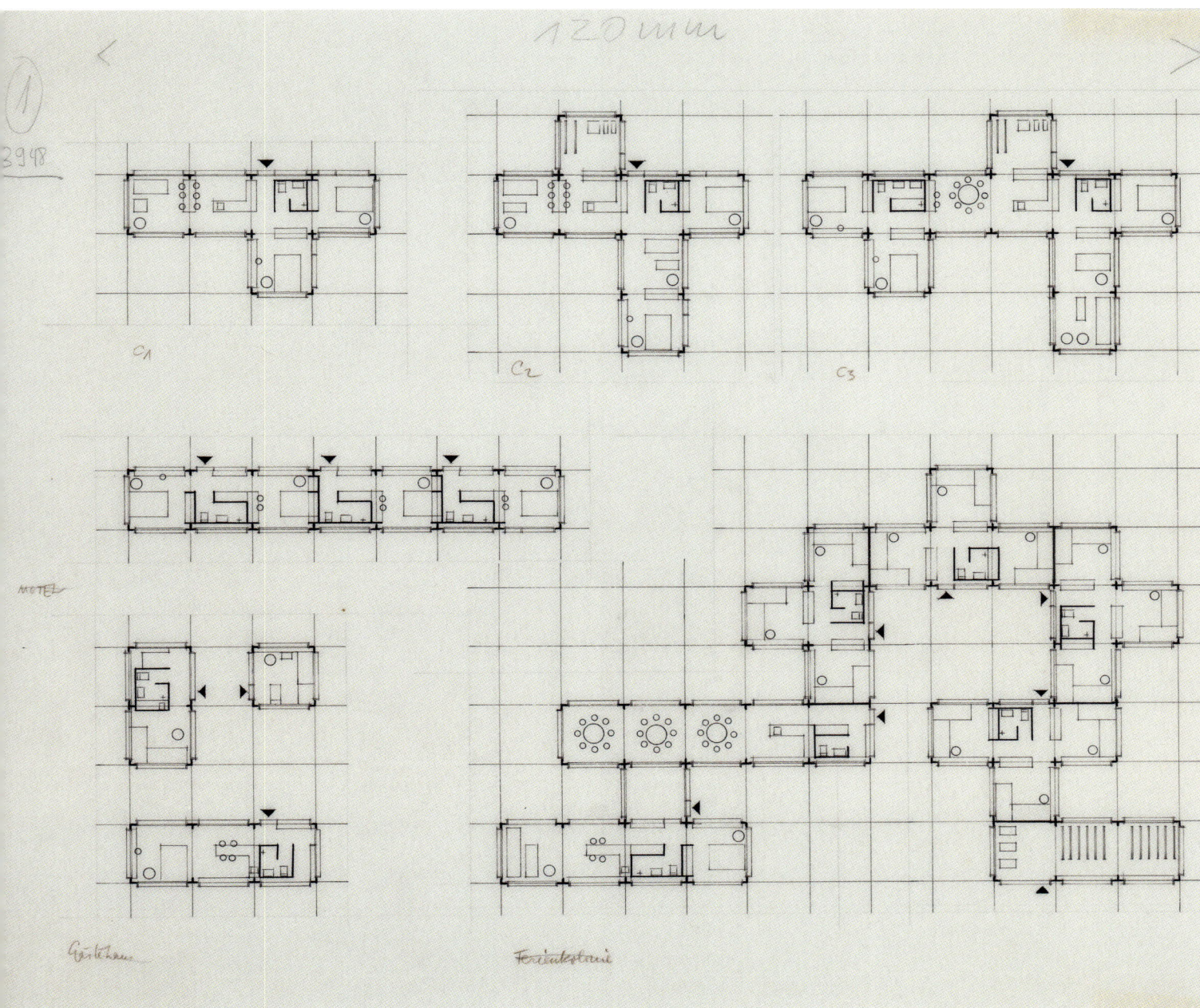

← Verner Panton and Arne Jacobsen met at the Cologne furniture fair in 1970, where Panton exhibited his *Visiona 2* project, which he had designed for the German chemical company Bayer AG and saw the launch of a new synthetic textile. This exhibition generated so much media attention that Jacobsen flew to Cologne to see for himself what his old employee had created. In this way, Jacobsen always tried to keep up with the latest developments in the profession.

↓ A sketch for a synagogue in Oxford, drafted by Jacobsen. It was his only religious building that was likely to be built and would have marked a return to his Jewish heritage. After his death, the project was handed over to other architects, although parts of Jacobsen's basic plan were preserved.

There were still problems with *Kvadraflex* and *Kubeflex*. The show houses should be completely finished by now. There was a lot of work involved, because these were building systems that could be added to infinitely. Furthermore, there were two different systems involved. At the design studio, they had sketched out every possible combination, ranging from single-family homes to holiday camps for children. So even though the prototype was a family-friendly villa, the details had to be ironed out. The sales material was also not yet finished, and the design studio had not yet been paid for the project by the client. For now, it was an investment on Jacobsen's part. The aim of the project was to boost the design studio into the market for cheap detached houses, which were currently popping up everywhere on the outskirts of the larger Danish cities. It marked a new direction for Jacobsen, where he finally combined his two core competencies into one. The house was a design, and the design a house.

Across the three design studios in Copenhagen and at the office in Newcastle, more than 70 architects were now working on major building projects. There was a hotel and shopping centre in Newcastle, the synagogue in Oxford, and the embassy in London. There were the two national banks, one in Copenhagen and one in Kuwait. The major German projects – Mainz City Hall and Castrop-Rauxel Town Hall, in addition to the Fehmarn holiday complex, which also required his input. A large villa for the rector of Roskilde University Centre, Erling Olsen, was also on the drawing board. It was intended to have vaulted roofs, as Le Corbusier might have designed it, but this was a Jacobsen composition that no one had seen yet. At the same time as this villa, the design studio won the competition for the new Roskilde University Centre – a building that also ushered in new forms and aesthetics in terms of the soft and plastic roundness that was so popular around 1970.

On this winter's day, Jacobsen still hadn't had his fill of new projects. He was probably a little overworked. There were many balls in the air. Tired, he sat down to study the incoming competition programmes. One in particular caught his eye. A new large cultural centre in the middle of Paris: Centre Georges Pompidou. He wanted to win it.

The design projects helped him to relax. Just one month earlier, he had agreed with the porcelain factory Bing & Grøndahl that he would design tableware for use in hotels and restaurants. There were 28 components on the list, so it was to be a large and varied series.

Jacobsen was very keen for this project to get off to a good start. He saw it as a follow-up and perhaps a conclusion to the series and shape-universe he had previously designed with *Cylinda Line* and *AJ cutlery*. Towards the afternoon, he came down the stairs of the design studio on Svanemøllevej, tired. His highly valued design collaborator, Teit Weylandt, sat sketching a reversible plate that could be used both as a deep plate on one side and as a flat plate on the other. They batted around some ideas. What should be the main concept? Jacobsen designed an asymmetrical plate. It was his last drawing.

He drove home, and even though the route along Strandvejen was straight and short, it felt strangely long. His chest felt tight and he wanted a rest. Exhausted, he crawled around the exercise bike that was on the landing. He knew very well that he should slow down and exercise more – the doctor had told him often enough. The exercise bike stood there like an evil spirit, trying to lure him in with its handlebars and pedals. An hour later he woke up with severe chest pain. Jonna called the ambulance, and Jacobsen was taken to Gentofte County Hospital, where he died that same evening at ten o'clock.

It was one of the first pieces of news read on the television the following day – "Architect Arne Jacobsen has died at the age of 69". Otto Weitling received the message by phone – he was in Germany for negotiations. But as Otto Weitling said: "The work continued, everyone worked independently and knew what to do. But we had lost our mentor and inspirational force." The next six months, however, were quite transformative for the design studio. How was the work actually to be continued? As the design firm had grown in recent years, the pressure on it as a professional organisation had also grown. It was only a few months ago that Arne Jacobsen, Otto Weitling, and Hans Dissing had discussed how a future partnership could work and how many partners the design firm should have going forwards.

It was Jacobsen's good friend for many years, Nils Koppel, who prepared the estate inventory. What had been completed and at what stage were all the construction projects? There were many construction projects underway, so there was more than DKK 25 million in fees owed by the design firm to the heirs. This corresponds to fees of more than DKK 200 million at 2023 prices. In addition, there was always ongoing work for Novo and healthy royalty income from Louis Poulsen and Fritz Hansen in particular, who had also put in the man-hours on the construction projects to ensure that they lived up to Jacobsen's standards. Finally, there were the properties on Svanemøllevej and parts of the Bellavista building. Arne and Jonna Jacobsen were extremely wealthy.

Otto Weitling was asked to take over the design firm alone, but chose to enter into a partnership with Hans Dissing, and the design firm Dissing+Weitling was born.

Being an architect is a liberal profession with all that it entails in terms of work in progress that must be completed even if the creator dies. When Alvar Aalto died, his wife kept the design studio open to complete the building projects before closing it down – the spirit could not be recreated. Zaha Hadid Architects continues in the spirit of the late founder and continues to design new projects in her name, which have become a brand in themselves and probably more relevant now than they were then. When Jacobsen died, both his family and Otto Weitling wanted a line to be drawn and for a renewal to take place. This was marked, among other things, by changing the name of the design studio to Dissing+Weitling.

However, Dissing+Weitling did not take over the design aspect. The Bing & Grondahl tableware was considered unfinished. The new toilets from Ideal Standard were also discontinued. There were no more Arne Jacobsen chairs. No more Arne Jacobsen lamps. A number of design agreements had been signed with new, international companies right up to Jacobsen's death, but these promising collaborations were also cancelled. The lawyer representing the estate was actually both quite negative about the valuation and pessimistic about the estate's chances of achieving proper royalty income in the future. His final remark on the estate statement was: "It will prove impossible to continue to collect license fees on the scale of those collected in the period 1968-1970." He was wrong.

Hans Dissing (right) and Otto Weitling took over the design studio after Jacobsen's death in 1971 and continued it, although not in the master's name, but as Dissing+Weitling. This architectural firm is still alive and well.

The basis for Dissing+Weitling was, of course, the completion of all of Jacobsen's buildings. But already in its first year, the design studio distinguished itself independently by winning prestigious competitions in West Germany, including an art museum for North Rhine-Westphalia and a spacious headquarters for IBM in Hamburg. The studio retained Jacobsen's elegance and style, and later became known for its bridges, including the Great Belt Bridge and the Øresund Bridge. Only with the completion of the National Bank of Denmark in Copenhagen seven years later was the last stone laid on an Arne Jacobsen building.

Over the years, Dissing+Weitling has had a design department led by Teit Weylandt and Hans Dissing, whose tasks were primarily within industrial design and product design. Dissing+Weitling was also involved in the development of the very first Novo pen and has since made a number of medical devices. But they did not continue Jacobsen's practice of creating striking interior design on a large scale for offices and homes. However, the design studio did achieve greater success in one area with a broad-based design, namely the *Air* titanium glasses. The starting point was Hans Dissing's irritation with his own bifocal glasses, and in collaboration with the company Lindberg Optik in Aarhus, glasses were developed in thin titanium wire, where all the small hinges were incorporated into the extremely minimalist frame.

Jacobsen's contour furniture for Fritz Hansen is his signature product, and probably the strongest products he created. They seem to be timeless. Like other 20th-century architects, it is a single signature series that has made Jacobsen especially famous, with products that will outlive their creator by many decades. This contrasts to the architectural culture, where Jacobsen's buildings are admired as unique works and, in many cases, have long since been protected. Mies van der Rohe and Alvar Aalto stuck to their design expression and changed it only slightly, but Gunnar Asplund and Arne Jacobsen followed the spirit of the times and continuously adapted to it. They changed their expressions when the time was right and followed their impulses. The buildings had a completely different foundation and framework of understanding than their design work. Jacobsen changed his architectural style several times and expressed himself in several different styles and design languages as the era dictated.

He started with traditional half-timbered brick houses. At the same time, he built in a white-painted functionalist style with flat roofs. He then switched to a restrained modernism in the pre-war town and city halls. In his own house after the war and in *Alléhusene* in Jægersborg, he switched to sculptural brick finishes in the early 1950s. A little later, but still in the same era, he ventured into glass facades and curtainwall buildings with Rødovre Town Hall and the Royal Hotel. Times change, and he transitions into brutalism with St Catherine's College and the unrealised Lyngby swimming pool, finally rounding off with an almost space age-like design with the Danish embassy in London and the also-unrealised Roskilde University Centre.

His design expression cannot be sharply divided into the eras. The furniture can be divided into three groups – furniture made specifically for the construction commissions of the 1930s, the timeless success stories of the 1950s, and the more fashionable furniture of the 1960s, none of which are still in production

at the time of writing (2023). In the 1960s, he arguably met with success more so with his industrial design, such as *Cylinda Line* and *Vola*. On the other hand, Arne and Jonna understood that textiles waxed and waned in their fashionability, and so they had to constantly keep that part of the company alive by inventing new things. A textile can be a hit one year and disappear from the market the next.

In the last ten years, it has been a trend for Danish design companies in particular to reproduce furniture designs from the 1930s and 1950s. Products have been revived only to lose momentum again, because the zeitgeist is constantly moving and sometimes quite quickly. We can see how a relaunch of Vilhelm Lauritzen's *Radiohus* furniture and other similar series quickly run out of steam, and this is typical of our time, where design seems to be a perpetual search for a new vision. Even more short-lived is the newly designed furniture that tries to copy without it being too obvious that they are copying. These almost-new creations must live as more-or-less fleeting snapshots of time in the stream of innovation, perhaps even produced abroad in inferior quality. At the time of writing in 2023, we're moving towards a repeat of the "plastic fantastic" world of the 1960s. This is where Verner Panton and the Italians reside with an expression that they have stuck true to their entire lives, and it is a long way from the Danish Modern of the 1950s.

The Danes know Arne Jacobsen by heart, but abroad people barely know that he designed buildings. While the Royal Hotel is a Danish masterpiece, for others it is just a high-rise building. Without knowing his name, many people around the world will recognise Jacobsen's contour furniture from the 1950s. And some may even be able to name a few of them – the *Swan*, the *Egg*, and the *Ant*. But the man behind it? Probably not. It is the very shape of the chair, the lamp, the cutlery, and Jacobsen's other designs that live on. These are the unique works that remain monumental.